more praise for
Sixty Slices of Life ... on Wry

"Under the irrepressible humor is a study in resilience, a recipe for success, and a delightful life story beginning with Buster, a dog who taught Fred the value in being completely and utterly himself."
—Jerri Strozier, Life Stories, Inc.

"Fred Flaxman offers up his recipe for *Sixty Slices of Life ... on Wry*: half wit and one or two grains of wisdom. Makes a good midnight snack."
—Cal Thomas, public TV executive

"*Sixty Slices of Life on Wry* mirrors the creative personality of Fred Flaxman, a character comfortable with his ethnic roots and secure enough in his beliefs to poke honest but gentle humor at himself while living his convictions. A delightful read where I identified with his reflections on many of life's profound questions."
—Sara Margaret Mitchell Rhodes,
    author, *A Slender Volume of Poems, Essays and Short Stories*

"Fred Flaxman is a talented humorist, and this is an enjoyable and readable book."
—Cleve Mathews,
    founding news director of National Public Radio

"Evrything I lerned about humer I lerned from Fred Flaxman."
—Peter Bradley, unemployed proofreeder

SIXTY SLICES OF LIFE...
ON WRY

The Private Life of a Public Broadcaster

BY FRED FLAXMAN

Story Book Publishers
Weaverville, North Carolina, USA

STORY BOOK PUBLISHERS, JANUARY 2010

Copyright © 2009 and 2010 by Fred Flaxman

All rights reserved. No part of this book may be reproduced or transmitted in any form or by any means, electronic or mechanical, including photocopying, recording, or by any information storage and retrieval system, without the written permission of the publisher, except by a reviewer quoting brief passages in a magazine, newspaper, or electronic medium.

Published and printed in the United States of America.
Library of Congress catalog card number 2009912407.

ISBN: 978-1-891513-01-5

Cover illustration by Brittany Jencks.
Cover design by Teleflax Productions.

edited by Fred Flaxman:

The Timeless Tales of Reginald Bretnor
Story Book Publishers, 1997

Dedicated to those whose slices of life, past and present, have made this tongue-in-cheek memoir possible, especially my mother, father, brothers, dog, cats, wife and children.

— *Fred Flaxman*

𝕭lessed are they who can laugh at themselves, for they shall never cease to be amused.

— a plaque offered for $16.50 on page 11 of the *Wireless* Holiday 1996 catalog "for fans and friends of public radio"

About the Author

Fred Flaxman is the producer and presenter of *Compact Discoveries*, a classical music public radio series heard on stations from Manila in the Philippines, through Eugene, Oregon, to Palm Beach, Florida. He is an award-winning writer, public television and radio producer, and public broadcasting executive.

His articles have appeared in the *New York Times, Washington Post, Wall Street Journal, Chicago Tribune, San Francisco Chronicle, San Francisco Examiner, Baltimore Sun, Houston Post, San Diego Union-Tribune, Seattle Times, Palm Beach Post, Sacramento* and *Parenting* magazines, among other publications. He is the recipient of a first-place award from the National Society of Newspaper Columnists. Some of his work has been translated and published in Europe.

Flaxman was the editor of *The Timeless Tales of Reginald Bretnor*, a collection of 15 stories by the late nationally published science fiction and fantasy author.

Flaxman was an occasional commentator for the nationally syndicated public radio programs *Marketplace* and *MonitorRadio*. His commentaries were also heard throughout southern Oregon and northern California on Jefferson Public Radio's daily newsmagazine program.

Flaxman was vice president for national programming of WTTW/Chicago for six years. There he was in charge of *A Child's Christmas in Wales*, which received nine international awards. He was also responsible for *Solti at 75: A Celebration; In Search of Love with Leo Buscaglia,* and several other PBS specials and series. He also started the annual *Illinois Young Performers Competition* with the Chicago Symphony Orchestra, and he received an Emmy award as executive producer of Marian Marzynski's *Messenger to Poland.*

In 1978 Flaxman founded Public Broadcasting International, headquartered in Paris, France, which, over the years, produced several major specials for PBS: *From Paris with Love: An Evening of French Television; An Evening of Belgian Television; Made in Taiwan: TV from the Republic of China;* and *PrimeTime/Japan,* starring Harry Anderson.

In 1970 Fred Flaxman was the founding manager of public radio station WETA-FM in Washington, D.C. He later served as a vice president of WETA-TV and as assistant general manager and director of programming and production for KUAT-TV, the public television station in Tucson, Arizona.

In 1991 Flaxman became general manager of Southern Oregon Public Television, Inc., a position he left in September, 1992, to work as an independent producer and freelance writer.

He was vice president for development of public broadcasting stations WXEL-TV-FM-DT, West Palm Beach, Florida, from April 27, 2000, until December 30, 2005.

Raised in the New Jersey suburbs of New York City, Flaxman holds a B.A. with honors in journalism from the University of Michigan, an M.A. in political science from Stanford University, and a certificate in French studies from the Sorbonne, University of Paris.

Defying modern precedent, he married his one and only wife, Annick Story Flaxman of Dinard, Brittany, France, in 1963. They have two children: Michael and Tana.

Contents

New Jersey

1	A Dog's Life	3
2	Why My Mom Was So Good to Me	5
3	The Buster Walk Jamboree	7
4	Buster's Bark and Bite	11
5	Puppy Love	13
6	A Whale of a Bet	16
7	A Donation from Murder, Inc.	20
8	My Criminal Career	23
9	The Banana that Left the Bunch	25
10	A Drugstore Education	30
11	The Fat of the Meat	33
12	The Shadow Knows	38
13	Buster and the Rats	40
14	Inventing the Portable TV Camera	43
15	The Kiss of Death	45
16	Sink or Swim	48

Michigan

17	Coke Caps and Classics	57
18	Getting High with Eleanor	60
19	Room for Rent; Will Accept Whites	63

France

20	Incident of Anti-Semitism	69
21	France Was Years Ahead	71
22	Love Par Avion	75

New York / Virginia

23 A Better Way to Make Babies	87
24 Necktie Nightmares	91
25 A Unique Memorial to Uncle Bill	96
26 Saying "No" to TV	101
27 Introducing the Classics	104

Washington, D.C.

28 Barcarolle No. 1	109
29 Birth of a Station	111
30 Renee Chaney & the Police	114
31 Support for Public Radio	116
32 The Saturday Night Massacre	118
33 Christmas in August	120
34 Steambath	122
35 My Dinner with Bibi	125

France Again / Bulgaria

36 From Paris with Love	133
37 The French Connection	141
38 French Fried in Belgium	144
39 Bulgarian Diplomacy	148
40 Gastronomically Challenged	152
41 Mischief in Paris	156

Arizona / Illinois

42 Meow Tse-Tung	161
43 Cat Calls	162
44 In Pursuit of "Pure" Gasoline	164
45 No Soliciting	167
46 A Real Test of American Citizenship	170
47 The Teen Disease	174

California / Oregon

48	Sixty Days as a Columnist	179
49	Chicken!	184
50	The Hen Who Loved Haydn	189
51	Potbellied Pigs… and Husbands	193
52	Mouth-Watering Meatless Meatballs?	197
53	Dealing with Dental Guilt	201

Florida / North Carolina

54	Sharing the Fruit of Our Labor	207
55	Speeding to Success	213
56	Dressing Appropriately	217
57	Selecting the Worst President in History	221
58	In Defense of Dishwashing	226
59	Exorcising the Evil Cholesterol Spirits	229
60	A Shocking Discovery	232

Acknowledgments

Many thanks to my wife, Annick, who was my first editor and proofreader, for helping to make this book much better than it would have been otherwise.

Thanks, as well, to the rest of my family (including my children, Prof. Michael Flaxman and Tana Flaxman Jencks; my late mother, Helen; and my brothers, John and Andrew) for supplying some of the memories I used, for their good attitude at sometimes being the subject of this material, and for their suggestions for improvements. Special thanks to granddaughter No. 1, Brittany Jencks, 19, for the cover illustration, and to granddaughter No. 2, Kaitlin Jencks, 12, for—as Mister Rogers used to say—"being you!"

Sincere thanks also to my friends and relatives who served as my "test market": my nieces, Caroline and Laura; my nephew, Gary (Flaxpeople all); Ramiro Arguello, George Bauer, George Blecher, Anne Bodin, Jim Bradley, Peter Bradley, Gerry Cavanaugh, Ken Droscher, John Friedman, Jim Jaffe, Steve Jencks, Peter Kreutzer, Marion LaTorre, Toby Levine, Tiffany Liong, Marian Marzynski, Karl Miller, Walter Meyer, Grace Shafir, Art Stevens, and George and Christine Waleski.

This book was many years in the making. Others who helped or encouraged me along the way, sometimes without realizing it, include Stephen Boyd, the late Leo Buscaglia, Jon Glascoe, Don Hall (the screenwriter who taught me how to spell "wry," not the poet whose classes I sometimes audited with the greatest pleasure at the University of Michigan), Richard Marschner, Ed Menaker, Bill McCarter, Joseph Pierson, Robert E. Simon, Jr., and Jim Vesely.

New Jersey

1
A Dog's Life

If you want your young child to learn responsibility, get him a dog. That's what conventional wisdom teaches. And that's been true in my case. But Buster also taught me more about *ir*responsibility than any human I've ever encountered.

When I was eight, I convinced my mother, who hated animals, to buy me a beagle. We got 50 percent off on Buster because he had stiff hind legs and undescended testicles. It taught my mom to be wary of bargains.

Buster lasted for 14 years and died of old age with a little assistance from the veterinarian and the approval of my mother. During his last few flatulent years, my mother took care of him completely since, by that time, I was away in college.

But for 10 years I walked Buster twice a day—in rain, snow, or shine, like an old-fashioned mailman. I fed him, brushed him, petted him and took care of him. I also confided in him, and he became my best friend.

I learned to be a responsible adult, just as conventional wisdom predicted. I married and had two children. For more than four decades I went to work each day, putting up gracefully with rush hours, boring meetings, budgets and personnel problems caused, presumedly, by employees who were deprived of dogs when they were children.

Sixty Slices of Life… on Wry

I footed the bills for my family's food, clothing, shelter, and college education. I even paid for their mistakes. I washed and dried the dishes and occasionally made the bed. I contributed to the United Way, supported the American Cancer Society, and worked as an executive for five non-profit, educational, public television stations. I don't think I could have been much more responsible.

But, all along, I harbored a secret desire to lead the good life Buster introduced me to. He never put in a full day's work. He never even worked part time. He never earned a dime, never did anything useful, never married or had children or knew or cared if he did, never put up with traffic, never sat through a meeting, never prepared a budget, never read a book or newspaper, never washed a car, never wasted time watching television—even public television—and never worried about nuclear war or anything else for that matter except, perhaps, which tree he should choose for his next stop. And even that he did without first obtaining an environmental impact report.

Buster was beautifully, innocently, and completely irresponsible. And I loved him as he was, for what he was.

My former colleagues at work would be surprised to learn that all I ever really wanted out of life was to have my back scratched while sitting in front of the TV, like Buster; to run free in the woods on a sunny summer day; and to curl up in front of a fire on a cold winter's evening, listening to classical music that someone else would put on the stereo.

Having a dog for 14 years may have taught me how to be responsible. But Buster taught me how to live.

2
Why My Mom Was So Good to Me

Every seven years, Mother's Day and my birthday fall on the same Sunday. This is altogether fitting because they really celebrate the same event. Without birthdays, after all, there would be no Mother's Days. Without mothers there would be no birthdays.

It seems to me we've been treating birthday anniversaries all wrong in our society. Birthday cakes and presents should be given to the mother of the person whose birthday anniversary we are celebrating, not to the person who was born. After all, the birthee had very little to do with the situation at the time compared to the birthor (or is it the birthess?)!

In any case, I don't need Mother's Day to honor my mom. I appreciate her all year long.

My mother taught me never to do anything that I would be ashamed to see on the front page of *The New York Times* (a lesson that former President Clinton's mother evidently didn't teach him). Although the *Times* has published a couple of my articles, I have yet to appear on the front page as a result of anything I have done which I am ashamed of—or proud of, for that matter.

My mother also taught me to be honest, but not exactly by example. We lived just one and a half miles south of the George Washington Bridge, and she went across it to Manhattan several times a month for shopping, attending

Sixty Slices of Life... on Wry

art classes, and visiting with friends. She would buy a book of tickets from the Port Authority which were designed to save money for commuters who used the bridge twice a day. The tickets would last only a month.

At the end of the month she would have tickets left over, and she would try using these tickets the next month instead of buying new ones. When the ticket takers noticed, she would apologize for not seeing the expiration date and pay the full fare: 50 cents in those days. When the ticket takers didn't notice, she crossed for nothing.

This is how I learned that it is perfectly OK for an honest person to stiff the Port Authority—or any Authority. But my mother would never take advantage of a little guy.

Although I adored my mother, I have to admit that she wasn't 100 percent perfect. I can even remember quite clearly the last time she did something really wrong. It was in 1944 when I was only four. She cooked a hamburger for me (which was about the limit of her cooking ability), and seasoned it with a pinch of pepper. I love hamburgers, and still do, but I hated pepper. I could detect a single grain of the seasoning on my food, and still can.

I refused to eat the hamburger.

Greatly annoyed, my mother insisted I swallow every morsel of the pepper-infested meat. So I got up from the table and ran out of the kitchen and downstairs to the basement game room. My mother followed in hot pursuit, chasing me around and around the ping-pong table with a paddle in one hand, a raised fist in the other. But she couldn't catch me.

"Stop!" she shouted, "and I won't spank you."

I stopped. And she gave me a good paddling. But her conscience must have bothered her, because she was very good to me for the rest of her 97-year long life.

3
The Buster Walk Jamboree

I have been producing programs for broadcast for over a half-century. At the height of my career I was in charge of creating PBS specials from France, Belgium, Taiwan, Japan, and Czechoslovakia, as well as the dramatic adaptation of Dylan Thomas's prose-poem, *A Child's Christmas in Wales*. But this all started when I was eight years old with a 15-minute program called *The Buster Walk Jamboree*. I was not only the producer, director, and host, I was the entire studio orchestra, conductor, and soloist.

The series was broadcast live, twice daily—three times a day on weekends. The time varied a bit because each show began when my dog, Buster, and I left the back door of our house in Palisade, N.J., continued while we walked around the block, and concluded only when we returned to the house. We stopped frequently along the way when Buster needed to sniff a tree, a fire hydrant, or something less aesthetically pleasing, and I needed to announce a commercial break.

The format was that of a 1940's musical variety show, which was not surprising, considering that it debuted in 1948. I was heard singing "Oh What a Beautiful Morning" from *Oklahoma!* I was heard playing the trumpet, violin, piano and drums, sometimes simultaneously. I was heard interviewing Rodgers and Hammerstein and delivering the commercials for Wheaties. The neighbors must have thought

Sixty Slices of Life... on Wry

I was off my rocker. But it made those incessant walks past the same houses, the same yards, and the same telephone poles pass much more quickly.

I rarely saw anyone else on these strolls. The sidewalks seem to have been made for me alone. Once in a while I would catch a glimpse of adult neighbors as they drove into their driveways and garages. There weren't many children my age, but one of these became my best friend, and one good friend was all I needed. Whenever I spotted him playing outside his house on the corner, *The Buster Walk Jamboree* would leave the air suddenly, only to pick up right where it left off once he was safely out of sight.

On nice weekend days in the spring, summer, and fall, there were *Buster Walk Jamboree* specials—half-hour, 45-minute, and one-hour programs when Buster and I left the immediate block behind and walked through the woods on the palisades. Going along the top of the cliffs, we had incredible views of the long, narrow town of Edgewater, N.J., below, of the Hudson River, and, on the other side, of the magnificent skyline of New York City.

Buster and I seemed to have had these woods to ourselves, rarely encountering anyone else on the narrow trails. Though we were just across the river from uptown Manhattan, we were in a totally different world, one which was filled with trees, wildflowers and little streams where I could find insects, if not bigger wildlife. Much to Buster's delight, squirrels were in abundance, but I don't ever recall seeing anything as large as a rabbit. Still, this was as close as I could come to nature in the nearest suburb of New York, and I adored it. Sometimes *The Buster Walk Jamboree* would even finish early, so that I could just sit on a rock and listen to the sounds of the stream passing by.

My mother would have been concerned had she known

Sixty Slices of Life... on Wry

how close to the edge of the cliffs I would venture. After all, she turned down the opportunity to buy a house right on the cliffs with magnificent, panoramic views, in favor of a home a half-block further inland, because she worried that one or more of her three young children would take the rapid route to Edgewater, some 350 feet below.

But I couldn't have fallen that far. There was a road that went between Palisade and Edgewater which weaved its way down the cliffs below these woods. When I stood on the edge, the road was about 50 feet below. One day when I was there with Buster and some schoolmates, someone thought it might be fun to see if we could hit the roofs of any of the cars on that road with stones we would take turns throwing. Fortunately, it was not an easy thing to do, and there were no winners. The game ended abruptly when one of the cars pulled over to the side of the road, a man got out, and ... (I don't know what he did, we got out of there so fast.)

The residents of Palisade wanted these woods preserved as a public park. Real estate developers, however, had other plans. My father joined a citizens' committee which successfully fought off the developers year after year for 18 years. Then one year they lost. It was my first lesson in "life is unfair." After all, is it fair when you have 18 wins and only one loss, and yet it is only the loss that counts, and it counts forever?

High-rise apartment buildings were constructed where *The Buster Walk Jamboree* was once broadcast for all the birds and bees of the palisades.

Not long afterwards my father had a stroke which half paralyzed him for the rest of his life. He could no longer climb the stairs of our house on Bluff Road. The family home was sold to my brother Andrew and his wife and my parents moved to one of the very apartment buildings

Sixty Slices of Life... on Wry

my father had fought so long and hard to keep from being constructed.

"If you can't beat 'em, join 'em."

Now my father, my woods, my dog, and *The Buster Walk Jamboree* are just memories of the increasingly distant past.

But I still make radio programs, although I no longer sing or provide my own orchestral accompaniment. The neighbors probably still think I'm a bit off my rocker, even though they are different neighbors in a different part of the country. And I've never owned another dog.

4
Buster's Bark and Bite

Buster had one very annoying habit. He was an incessant barker. He barked when anyone came to the house. He barked when there was no one around at all. He barked to go out. He barked to come back in. He barked whenever the milkman came to deliver milk. He barked whenever the mailman came with the mail. But when my older brother returned in the middle of the night without his keys one time, none of his knocking on doors or windows managed to get Buster to bark, of course, because he was fast asleep.

Worst of all, Buster barked continuously when he was out on his leashed runway in the back yard, disturbing everyone in the neighborhood within range of his piercing sounds. And he had a very extensive range.

So, once in a while, we broke the law and let him run loose. On more numerous occasions he broke the law himself and dashed out of the house when someone came in.

I remember one such instance when Buster made his way around the block and up the next street to Judge Aronsohn's house where he dined on son Richard's pet chickens.

I understood even at that young age that a judge was responsible for upholding the law. So when I heard what had happened, I spent days trying to avoid the police, certain that, as Buster's owner, I was going to be arrested.

Sixty Slices of Life... on Wry

But I needn't have worried. Having chickens in the suburbs was just as much against the law as letting your dog run loose.

As it happens, both Richard Aronsohn and I graduated the same private high school, the Horace Mann School for Boys. Many years later, in 1994 to be exact, the following item appeared in the class notes of the Horace Mann Alumni Magazine:

1956
> After reading the spring issue of the HM magazine, **Richard Aronsohn** sent this note: "I read with pleasure the fact that Fred Flaxman ('58) made his debut as an occasional commentator on Monitor Radio with a piece about what he learned about work from his dog, Buster... Buster assassinated my six Easter chickens."

I got Richard's address from the Alumni Association and wrote him immediately:

"Buster, I'm sure, was just trying to uphold suburban Fort Lee's ordinance against farm animals and poultry," I said. "He obviously felt less attached to the town's leash law, but, hey, it's a dog's life, after all."

But I guess Richard must have agreed with the mailman and all sorts of delivery men that, as bad as Buster's bark was, his bite was even worse.

5
Puppy Love

Buster's physical handicap prevented him from siring offspring, but didn't diminish his desire to try. So he had an affair with a mongrel who lived on the other side of the busiest street in town. Each time Buster went out, I worried that it would be his last, that a car would get him as he crossed Palisade Avenue. He never learned to look both ways before crossing a street. Or anything else, for that matter.

Several times a year we got calls that Buster had been found on the other side of the avenue. But the calls were always from the pound, whose dogcatchers had picked up Buster in the best of health on his way to visit his girl friend.

I always wondered how they caught him. Despite his stiff legs, Buster could have won the 100-meter race if there had been a Special Olympics for handicapped canines.

When I was 13 I started Horace Mann and Buster was sent into exile. My mother, sick and tired of a dog who wouldn't stop barking and who never even learned to be housebroken, gave him away.

I was so miserable, my mother made an appointment with the headmaster of Horace Mann to seek his advice as to what she should do about me. I was not present at this meeting and didn't even know that it was taking place. So it came as a big surprise to me later when I learned that

Sixty Slices of Life... on Wry

Dr. Gratwick strongly recommended that my mother get Buster back.

Giving away Buster was like getting rid of one of my brothers, he told her. Of course that wouldn't have bothered me half as much.

When she returned from her appointment, my mother found me in my room crying on my bed, photos of Buster spread out before me.

We picked my favorite beagle up the next day.

Buster helped me get through my difficult teenage years. He didn't care what grades I got, whether or not I was elected class president, how many times I skipped physical education, whether or not I did my homework, how well I understood algebra, or what college I would go to. He was always there, ready to listen, full of sympathy. He was a constant source of unconditional love, which I needed even more than he did.

But Buster remained a dog, of course, and I was developing an interest in girls. Although he had beautiful, soft tan, black and white fur, a slender body with large, floppy ears, and a long, attractive black tail with a white tip that he used successfully to express every mood from happiness to fear, he lacked certain features which were becoming more and more important to me for reasons I didn't fully understand.

But girls were not a part of my everyday world. The private school I went to was for boys only. So were the summer camps I was sent to. I had two brothers but no sisters. Even Buster was a male. My curiosity about the female of the species couldn't have been greater, and my chances of meeting one couldn't have been less.

I was too isolated to meet public school girls from my neighborhood, too young to drive, too busy trying to keep

Sixty Slices of Life... on Wry

up with my school work to go out weekends.

Yet I wanted so badly to see what a woman looked like under all those girly clothes. *Playboy* didn't exist yet. There was no pill. I was becoming a man, but the only warm, soft body I could pet was Buster's.

Eventually I got my driver's license, began dating, and found a partially willing girl friend. It was only then that I learned that puppy love has nothing to do with young dogs.

6
A Whale of a Bet

I am not a gambler, and there are good reasons for this. When I was about five I made the first—and last—substantial bet of my life. At least I don't think I'll make another wager until I've somehow managed to pay off this one. And that might take a while.

My oldest brother, John, said that a whale was a mammal. I, of course, knew that was ridiculous. And I put my money where my mouth was. Trouble is, my mouth was bigger than my wallet, and I still owe him a million dollars.

I learned two lessons from this experience:

(1) Never bet against older brothers.

(2) Whales are not fish, despite all evidence to the contrary.

At the time John advised me never to bet on anything unless I was 100% sure that I was correct. I have not been 100% sure of anything since.

I had a horse-racing game when I was a little older and I loved playing it with my best friend down the street. Although we bet on each race, we used play money and I knew it wasn't for real. Then, too, that was not my favorite part of the game. What I liked most was thinking up names for my horses, and announcing each race for my imaginary radio station, WFBC, the Flaxman Broadcasting Company:

"*Spaghetti King* and *Pepto Dismal* are falling behind *Gildersleeve* and *Peanut Butter* as the herd starts into the final

Sixty Slices of Life... on Wry

stretch. But wait! Coming up rapidly from behind is the dark horse of the Doodoo Derby—*Nincompoop!"*

(*Nincompoop* was a name I knew well. My father used it often when I failed to live up to his expectations.)

Many years later I went to a real horse race for the first—and probably last—time. I couldn't get myself to bet real money on the results and, of course, nothing is as boring as a horse race if you don't care who wins.

More recently my wife and I passed through Reno, Nevada. We saw slot machines every place we looked there—in hotel lobbies, restaurants, even in men's rooms. I put four quarters in one of these armed bandits and lost my total gaming budget for the trip. I felt terrible the rest of the day.

Perhaps I'm just too cheap to be a gambler.

Nevertheless, when we first moved to southern Oregon, I almost convinced myself to make the second largest bet of my life (second only to the one I lost to brother John).

My wife and I found the most beautiful site to build our dream house—25 acres of woods on the top of a small mountain with a house site on a knoll where we would have 360° panoramic views of the towns, valleys, and mountains all around. The price was reasonable; the drive to town less than a half-hour. This property met all our criteria except one: there was no well.

Now I was certainly not going to purchase a property which might not have water on it. If there is one thing I simply cannot do without, it's my morning shower. So I asked if the owners would put in a well first, agreeing to sign a contract contingent on its producing at least five gallons a minute.

But the owners were selling the property precisely

because they desperately needed cash. They were, however, willing to sign a contract contingent on the well's producing a minimum of five gallons per minute—if my wife and I put up the non-refundable money for the drilling.

I started convincing myself that the only reason this gorgeous piece of property was still on the market was that no one had yet been willing to take that gamble. The people who did, and who were successful, would get as their reward the right to live on this heavenly site for the rest of their lives. Even forever, if they chose to be buried there, which is fine, according to Oregon law.

Our attorney advised us against taking this risk. He said the area had a reputation for lacking water, and a quick check of well records showed he was right. But he had told us, as well, that he, personally, wouldn't consider living beyond the city limits. "Even if you have well water to begin with," he said, "there is no guarantee it will last."

"Lawyers!" I told myself, "It's their business to be overly careful and not take chances, and to advise their clients to do the same." How could anyone other than a practical, aesthetically deprived attorney move to beautiful, mountainous southern Oregon and live in flat, ugly Medford?

So my wife and I had just about decided to sign on the dotted line… when I chickened out.

We ended up purchasing half as many acres with an even better view, on a property which was closer to town —and more expensive. But it came with a seven gallon-per-minute well.

A few weeks later, by pure coincidence, our attorney had another client who was interested in that very same well-less property. The new client signed the same contingency clause we had proposed. He ended up paying $7,500 for a well which produced less than a half-gallon a minute.

Sixty Slices of Life… on Wry

The land is probably still for sale today.

All this confirmed my non-gambling instincts. And they are reconfirmed every time I fill out one of those Publishers' Clearinghouse sweepstakes, wasting valuable time, not to mention postage.

If, instead of sending in these entries each time, I had given my brother John the money I spent on postage, I might have paid off my debt by now.

When I was "between jobs," not long after moving to southern Oregon, I used a dollar of my unemployment insurance to play the Oregon Lottery. I was hoping to win enough money to cover the hefty costs of buying individual health insurance. I should have just thrown that money in the convenience store's parking lot. That would have at least made someone else happy.

Perhaps it's good that I didn't win. It might have given me a guilty conscience. Money, after all, is supposed to be earned by hard work, creativity, and honest, socially-useful enterprise—not by chance.

I might just as well make my fortune by tricking five-year-olds who don't know the difference between a mammal and a fish. The odds, at least, would be in my favor.

Sixty Slices of Life... on Wry

7
A Donation from Murder, Inc.

Journalists thrive on corruption. Not their own, of course, but that of others—mostly politicians. I, for one, have never lived in any state where we had honest government—and I've lived in New Jersey, New York, Michigan, Virginia, Arizona, Illinois, California, Oregon, Florida, and North Carolina.

If, heaven forbid, we were to elect ethical representatives to the state assembly and senate, or honest, law-abiding sheriffs, what would local newspapers put on their front pages? Wedding announcements? Obituaries? Good news? Would any of that sell newspapers?

I grew up in one of the most corrupt areas of the country—New Jersey—and moved west after living for six years in a city where even the judges took bribes—Chicago.

My introduction to questionable governmental practices came when I was 10 and I went to get a haircut at Joe's Barber Shop in Palisade, N.J. While Joe was cutting my hair, a man walked in, came up to Joe, and said, *sotto voce:* "Two on Whirlaway in the fourth."

Joe stopped what he was doing, took the man's two dollars, and walked into the back room. He returned with a slip which he handed the man, who then left without even getting a trim.

Young as I was, I realized what was going on—I had a horse-racing game at home. I also knew—from listening

Sixty Slices of Life... on Wry

to all those crime programs on radio—that it was illegal to place off-track bets on races. I quickly put two and two together and concluded that my barber was a bookie.

I tried to keep my cool and to live with this new knowledge long enough to finish my haircut, walk home, and ask my mother to call the police. But, apparently this wasn't necessary. The police were already on to Joe. Even before he had finished with me, an officer of the law walked in. I held my breath in anticipation, expecting to watch poor old Joe arrested before my very eyes. I wondered who would finish my haircut. Then the policeman spoke:

"Two on Silverstreak in the sixth," he said. Joe took his two dollars to the back room and brought the cop a slip of paper.

When I got home, I told my mother to call the police.

"What good will that do?" she asked. "You said yourself that you saw a policeman place a bet there, too. The police already know that Joe's a bookie. They're using him to place bets themselves and making sure he isn't arrested."

I didn't get my hair cut at Joe's after that. Good thing, too. I might have been mowed down by accident when someone, presumedly from the Mafia or Murder, Incorporated, actually came in with a submachine gun and sprayed bullets all over an elderly gentleman with a musical Italian name while he was getting his hair cut. It made the front pages of the newspapers, of course. You don't expect them to put it with the obituaries, do you?

••••

Alberto Anastasia, whom the papers called the head of Murder, Incorporated, lived just down the street from us,

Sixty Slices of Life... on Wry

in a mansion on the cliffs overlooking the Hudson River and the New York skyline. He was a good, peaceful neighbor, evidently commuting to New York like most of the upright citizens of our community.

When I was about twelve, my mother volunteered to raise money for the American Cancer Society. She asked me to go door to door to collect from the neighbors. With some hesitation, I walked up Anastasia's long driveway, right past his two growling, but chained, Doberman pinschers, and rang his bell. I expected a servant or a bodyguard to answer, but Anastasia came to the door himself. I recognized him from his frequent photos on the front page.

"Would you like to contribute to the American Cancer Society?" I asked.

"I gives where I works," he replied.

I didn't ask where that was.

8
My Criminal Career

When I was 10 years old I committed the perfect crime. As that was more than a half-century ago and, presumably, the statute of limitations for burglary prohibits my punishment at this late date, I shall confess the whole sordid business for the first time.

My parents dragged me along with them to Preakness Hills Country Club every weekend during the golf season in New Jersey. I couldn't play golf and had no interest in the game, so I was very bored by these outings. This particular day was either before or after the swimming season, I don't remember which. But I recall very clearly that there was no water in the swimming pool, and I had absolutely nothing to do while my parents were on the course.

My mother had given me a couple of used, lifeless golf balls to occupy myself with, so I went to the pool area and made up a game which utilized the golf balls.

The deck was paved and for some reason, perhaps for drainage, there were little, perfectly round holes filled with pipe ends in the cement surface on each side of the rectangular pool. Alone next to the empty pool, I tried to roll the golf balls into those holes.

I don't remember how long it took me to get those balls in the holes, but I succeeded eventually—two right in a row. Then, much to my surprise and horror, I discovered I couldn't get the balls out again. The circumference of the

Sixty Slices of Life... on Wry

holes was just a bit wider than that of the balls, and both golf balls disappeared in those pipes which, for all I knew, went all the way to China.

I felt terrible. I had lost these two special, solid, white, pockmarked, stamped golf balls which my mother had entrusted to me for safekeeping. What could I do? What would I tell her? How, indeed, could I face her after what I had done?

Depressed, my head hanging down, I walked out of the pool area toward the golf course. I passed a small stand run by the pro shop where they sold hats, golf clubs, gloves, and other equipment for the game.

They had new golf balls in boxes wrapped in plastic. They also had an open box of used golf balls. I noticed that two of these used golf balls looked exactly like the two I had lost at the pool.

So when the man tending the stand looked the other way, I took those two golf balls, and gave them to my mother when she returned from her tournament. And I've felt guilty about what I did ever since.

I learned two very important lessons from that experience: (1) Crime pays. (2) The guilty feelings I got afterwards weren't worth the benefits.

My criminal career thus ended the same day it began, and I didn't grow up to be a thief even though I got away with my one and only robbery. My moral training took place at the side of an empty country club swimming pool rather than inside a half-empty Jewish synagogue or Christian church. But, believe me, I learned the same lesson from the Two Golf Balls that I might otherwise have received from the Ten Commandments.

9
The Banana That Left the Bunch

I was a skinny, nonstop-talking eight-year-old when my parents sent me away for the first time to a summer camp for budding athletes.

Camp Winaukee, on the banks of Lake Winnipesaukee in New Hampshire, was selected not because I was good at sports, but because my two older brothers were. My parents insisted on treating us all equally, whether we wanted to be treated equally or not.

Every camp day started out with compulsory calisthenics on the tennis courts just outside our cabins. The athletic director, who was undoubtedly an ex-Marine drill seargent, led these painful exercises, shouting out orders, mixed with words of wisdom about the importance of unquestioningly doing what we were told.

"You know what happened to the banana that left the bunch?" he asked retorically. "It got skinned."

I don't remember the athletic director's name or anything else he said that summer, but I have never forgotten what happened to the banana that left the bunch.

One morning, shortly after arriving at camp, I returned from the tennis courts to the wood plank cabin that was my temporary home, and penciled the very first letter I ever wrote. Its spelling may have been imperfect, but its logic was impeccable:

Sixty Slices of Life... on Wry

Dear Mother and Father,
I'm having a good time. I'll tell you what happend next post card. I can not tell you now becoss it is morning and I do not no what happen yet.
XXX *Love, Your son Fred* **XXX**

Well, afternoon eventually arrived, and what happened that day and every day was sports. Softball, tennis, volleyball, basketball—all kinds of ball games in which I obtained rapid notoriety for my lack of ability in catching balls, throwing balls, bouncing balls, and hitting balls.

Not being good at these activities—or swimming or running or anything else that required energy, coordination, and stamina—I naturally grew to dislike camp rather rapidly. Nevertheless, I continued to go each summer, not because it met my needs, I realize now, but because it met my parents' annual desire to have eight straight weeks without three young sons around.

(Much later, when I was grown, married, and with two children of my own, I would learn to appreciate the value of summer camps. But by the time that situation developed, these hot-weather juvenile incarceration centers had become so expensive, I could not afford to send my own children to one.)

By the time I was 11, though, I found some sports I could and did excel at. One was archery. This was the complete opposite of any other activity offered at the camp I had by then switched to: Camp Robinson Crusoe in Massachusetts. Instead of running or jumping or climbing or otherwise exerting myself to obtain some useless points for

Sixty Slices of Life… on Wry

a team, all I had to do to succeed was to stand still by myself, hold my breath, pull back a taut string with an arrow resting on it, and let go, aiming at a straw-filled plastic target exactly 15 yards away.

This I did well enough to earn "Junior Yeoman" and "Yeoman" diplomas from the Camp Archery Association of the United States in 1951. (Please forgive me for mentioning these high honors, but more than a half-century has passed since then and I have never before been able to make any use of them whatsoever. They didn't help me graduate elementary school or get into high school or college, never mind find a place on my résumé or get me a job. And sometimes I feel that 57 years is a long time to save totally useless certificates.)

The next summer—this time at Camp Mooselauke in New Hampshire—I was to prove even better at riflery. After all, I didn't even have to stand up for that.

Riflery was done lying down on a mattress, staying as still as possible, closing one eye, looking through the site with the other, and moving your second finger of your right hand slowly and carefully. If you did this correctly and didn't move at all, you could get the bullet you fired to hit the target in or very close to its bull's-eye.

Now there was a sport I could master, and I received a host of diplomas, awards and certificates from the National Rifle Association to prove it. I became a "Marksman," a "Marksman-First Class," a "Pro-Marksman," and a "Sharpshooter"—all in the single summer of 1952.

(I also discovered those certificates in a file. But I threw out the accompanying medals years ago when I realized that the NRA would just as soon people shot animals or other people as paper targets, and that the right to own a gun was more important to them than the right not to be shot.)

Sixty Slices of Life... on Wry

There was a third "sport" I excelled at—Ping-Pong. Because we had a Ping-Pong table in our basement at home, I had played the game as long as I could remember. My older brothers taught me how, and this was usually my game of choice if my friends insisted that we do something more energetic than playing with toy soldiers on the floor or sitting down at a card table for a relaxing game of "war."

I learned to play the least exhausting game of table tennis I could manage. My goal was to stand in one place and get my opponent running back and forth by hitting the ball first to one corner on his side, then to the other.

These activities may have marginally helped my self-esteem, but growing up masculine and American in the 1950s meant that, if you weren't good at softball, you were an inferior human being and should seriously consider suicide. So I still disliked camp and pleaded with my parents to let me stay at home each summer.

"You'll get bored," my mother would argue. "You won't know what to do with yourself all that time."

"Let me try it just once, mom," I would retort. "I'll bet you I'll be very happy at home."

Finally, at the age of 13, I got my wish. While the other kids were out playing ball, I stayed in my room at my desk trying to design the perfect city. It was called "Busterville," and my idea of the ideal urban environment was one which didn't have any stop signs or traffic lights. My cities had more clover-leaf interchanges than buildings. (Los Angeles stole all my designs.) Despite its name, Busterville had no features I can recall to benefit its canine population.

Except for a week when I accompanied my parents on a visit to Bermuda, I spent that entire summer on my own, loving every minute.

The following year I went out west with my parents on

Sixty Slices of Life... on Wry

a grand tour that included western Canada. I kept a diary in which I recorded a numerically, if not orthographically, accurate list of the animals I spotted each day:

> July 10, 1954
> We left Yellowstone this morning so here is my final account of the wildlife I have seen there:
> 34 bears
> 4 moose
> 1 dear
> 1 cyote
> 4 elk

I forced my parents to take me to every zoo in every city we passed. My diary shows that I had a wonderful summer. I'm sure I completely ruined theirs.

So, at 15, my parents sent me back to camp once again, but this time there was a big difference. I got to go to the National Music Camp at Interlochen, Michigan. There the values were totally different. The arts were important; athletics were not. Baseball was even prohibited, lest a young musician break a badly-needed, piano-playing finger. On the other hand, co-educational Interlochen featured one sport no all-boys camp I ever attended had at all—necking!

It was the one and only camp I ever liked.

10
A Drugstore Education

When I grew up in Palisade, the town's chief claim to fame was an amusement park. My house was two blocks north of the penny arcade, site of my first summer employment at age 13.

That job lasted only two weeks, not because I was fired but because my mother was too embarrassed to have me working with all that "riffraff." Lots of things embarrassed my mother. She was ashamed of living in New Jersey, ashamed that her immigrant parents spoke English with a foreign accent, ashamed of being Jewish—and mortified of being the mother of a son who gave out change in the penny arcade at Palisades Amusement Park.

So she spoke to Mr. Smalowitz at the drugstore a few blocks away at the old trolley track junction, and convinced him to give me a job for the summer. As the pay and working conditions were better than at the penny arcade, I was happy to switch. And, as it turned out, I learned more from this experience than how to make an ice cream soda.

One of my tasks was to go through all the magazines that came in and remove those which were on a list issued by the National Organization for Decent Literature. Magazines in 1953 were not nearly as revealing and as explicit as today, but the ones on the N.O.D.L. index certainly showed parts of the female anatomy I didn't see at home. Whenever I could, I sat in a corner of the stock room and conscientiously

Sixty Slices of Life... on Wry

looked through these magazines, making sure none of them reached the sales rack.

The drugstore furthered my education in other ways as well. I remember one day when a man came up to the counter, smelling of alcohol, and asked me for something which his slurred speech made incomprehensible. I must have looked puzzled.

"TwotinsofTrojans!" he repeated, a bit more loudly, but I still couldn't figure out where one word ended and the next began.

"I'm sorry, I don't understand you," I replied.

"TWO TINS OF TROJANS!" he shouted now, clearly and distinctly. 'PROPHYLACTICS! PROPHYLACTICS, BOY! WHAT'S THE MATTER WITH YOU?"

That's how I learned that Trojans were condoms. But several more years passed before I learned what condoms were.

The same man then went over to the soda fountain and I followed him, since, at that moment, I was the only one working aside from the pharmacist.

"What can I get you?" I asked politely, trying to make up for my ignorance at the front counter.

"A scotch on the rocks," he stammered.

"I'm sorry, sir, but we don't serve alcohol," I replied.

"Then get me a black and white malt," he said.

In a way, this was an even bigger problem for me than serving him a scotch on the rocks. At least I knew what that was and how to prepare it, since my father had one each day when he returned from work. But I couldn't remember what a black and white malt was for the life of me.

I excused myself for a moment and went into the stock room where I racked my brain, trying to remember

Sixty Slices of Life... on Wry

how to prepare his order. I had been given so many instructions about so many things in such a short time, the fountain recipes were becoming all muddled in my mind. But I was too embarrassed to admit that I needed help.

So I went back to the soda fountain and asked the inebriated customer how he liked his black and white malt —with a scoop of vanilla ice cream and a scoop of chocolate ice cream, or just chocolate ice cream with milk? Using this method, I worked the recipe out of him and gave him exactly what he wanted. And he enjoyed every last drop of his malt before he finally got up from the counter and walked out of the store—without paying his bill.

11
The Fat of the Meat

When all your housing, food, medical, and clothing costs are taken care of by your parents, it isn't too hard to save money for something *really* useful, even if you aren't making much to begin with.

That was my case at the end of the summer of my 13th year when I finished my work at the local drugstore. I used my entire savings account to purchase a reel-to-reel magnetic tape recorder.

By the time I had taken the machine out of its box and learned how to use it, my mother called me for dinner. So I went downstairs with my new recorder, quickly set it up under the dining room table, and pushed the "RECORD" button.

After dinner I added opening and closing announcements and theme music from a 45 rpm recording by Peewee Hunt and his band, creating, as it turned out, my very first radio program—the only one I ever made that was never broadcast.

I expected it to come out like *Ozzie and Harriet, Burns and Allen,* or perhaps even *The Goldbergs*. But the 1950s never really resembled those early TV shows. My experience, at least, was more like *Life with the Flaxmans* and that day's episode, "The Fat of the Meat."

The first voice on the tape after my opening was my father's, and he said something I doubt very much he would

Sixty Slices of Life... on Wry

have wanted to have been remembered by: "Get the fat out of those lamb chops even if they shrivel up. I don't care."

"All right," my mother replied, and you would have thought that the subject would have finished right then. But the discussion had just begun, and this turned out to be a half-hour show.

"I don't want any fat in the meat, so if this fat ... is there, I'd rather it come out of the meat," my father continued.

"I see," my mother replied. "Even if it shrivels up?"

"The fat will come out of the meat, which is what I want. I don't know the rest of the stuff and I'm not interested. There's enough fat in this meat. It isn't like the Jewish meat, the kosher meat, where they actually throw the fat out with the ... a ... with the salt. There's plenty of fat in this meat. Cut it off. Let it shrivel up. I don't want all this fat in the meat."

"You think that's what kosher meat does—takes the fat out of the meat?" my mother asked.

"Takes the blood out of it," my father responded.

"Well," my mother said, "blood and fat are entirely different things."

But my mother couldn't be allowed to win such an important point, so my father came quickly back to the meat of the issue, so to speak: "I know, it takes the ... the ... but basically there's enough meat, without the fat, which will give me enough food."

"You're ready to have it...," my mother went on, not being able to stop herself, but she got no further.

"I'm ready to have it even though it shrivels up!" my father proclaimed. "The meat is still there. See, the water gets out of the meat, the fat gets out of the meat or the blood gets out of the meat in that process. The meat is still there in concentrated form. It doesn't evaporate."

Sixty Slices of Life... on Wry

"Oh, that's what I was told that it does!"

"It evaporates?"

"It ... Yes. It burns up and you have no benefit of the meat. That's the whole point. I wouldn't care if it was in a different form. But I was told that the thing is just like ... if you eat carbon after something burns, is that just as beneficial as if you ate the thing without carbon? Just because it's in different form, is it just as beneficial? That's the point. When I say the meat is wasteful because ... it doesn't evaporate—that's not the word—but it does ... a ... whatever ... burns out, and when it burns out it isn't in the same form as the meat itself."

"I'm not talking about making charcoal out of the meat."

"No, that was just to give you an idea of what I mean."

"Yes, you want to stress something. I've made lamb chops and I've taken all of the fat off and I've liked it, see? It wasn't carbon."

"There's never any meat in that end that you ever want? There's always a strip in the middle."

"Oh, well, that strip in the middle! Well, you cut that off and have it for yourself if you like it! See, you're trying to tell me that you don't want to waste so much stuff. If you don't want to waste it ..."

"Because people eat this part."

"Well, maybe people do, so you eat it, see. I don't eat it. Freddy doesn't eat it. Now, if you like it ..."

"Buster will eat it."

"Well, give it to Buster. If you want to talk about saving it that's a different story."

"That's not what I meant in the first place ...," my mother went on.

Sixty Slices of Life... on Wry

"Well, I think that's your basic reason behind your mind that you don't want to express," my father responded with a sarcastic chuckle in his voice.

"That's exactly what I mean—your expressing an idea that I have ... and that you *think* I have!"

To which my father, who loved to tease my mother every chance he got, said caustically: "I think psychologically that's what's in the back of your mind. You hate to waste anything when you can put it down our stomachs. Your intestines are the best, and you hate to see it wasted. If Buster got it, it wouldn't be wasted so let Buster have it."

Ignoring that sensible proposal to end this dispute and talk about more important things, or even less important things, or, at least, *anything* else, my mother returned to her last point: "Even if you don't like that part of it, there's meat there, in between."

"Why don't you eat it?" my father suggested once again.

"I wouldn't eat a lamb chop, even the best part."

"You wouldn't eat ... but you would stuff our bellies ..."

"You're the ones who like lamb chops."

"Oh, I see, but you like to stuff our bellies with that stuff because you think it's wasted. So take this and ... and ... and if it's too solid for Buster, put it in the grinder and give it to Buster. Don't try to give it to us. Or throw it out. Do one of the two."

The last line went to my mother: "Buster will have a good meal," she said. "Here, Buster."

And the Flaxman Broadcasting System's presentation of *Life with the Flaxmans* drew to a close, the announcer—yours truly—giving the brief credits for "today's episode, 'The Fat of the Meat'."

Sixty Slices of Life… on Wry

As in the beginning, the bright, cheerful, pre-rock-and-roll music of Peewee Hunt played underneath my words, fading out at the end, just like a real radio program.

Nothing could have been more real than this "show." But it was never broadcast beyond our living room, and never played there again. Many years later, when my mother learned to her horror that the tape still existed, she wanted me to erase it. But I couldn't do that.

"The Fat of the Meat" might not show off my father's conversational skills at their best. It may not reflect his usual thoughtfulness, intelligence, and good sense of humor. He undoubtedly deserves a better audio legacy. But this is the one and only "radio program" we ever did together, and all these years after his death, this is the only recording which remains of my father's voice.

12
The Shadow Knows

When I was 7 years old, I started taking piano lessons—not because I wanted to, but because my mother wanted me to. She sat next to me on the piano bench every day encouraging me to practice. Her method was simple and direct. When I tried to leave, she hit me.

Despite my mother's efforts to turn me on to classical music, I can't honestly attribute my discovery of Brahms and Beethoven to her ... nor to my first piano teacher, who succeeded only in teaching me simple, boring pieces in C major.

No, when I was growing up in the 1940s, I learned to love Rossini, Liszt, Gounod, and their crowd from a group of nationally famous, inspired instructors. I can still remember their names: one was called "The Lone Ranger;" another, "Sergeant Preston of the Yukon;" a third, "The Shadow."

Each educator concentrated exclusively on teaching me just one part of one composition. This same excerpt was played over and over again, every week, at the beginning and end of each half-hour lesson. And all instruction was given at home, coming to me with the switch of a button, over the radio.

I was absolutely spellbound by these teachers and the fascinating stories they told. Oddly enough, these music instructors never talked about sharps and flats or treble and

Sixty Slices of Life... on Wry

bass clefs, and the tales they told never had anything to do with music. Nevertheless "The Lone Ranger" taught me Rossini's *William Tell Overture*. "Sergeant Preston" introduced me to the *Donna Diana Overture* by Reznicek. "The Shadow" scared me with sections of Lizst's *Les Préludes*.

Then TV came along, and with it, a new set of exciting classical music lessons. There was "The Big Story," in which newspaper reporters solved a different real-life mystery every Friday night, but which played the same exciting theme from Richard Strauss' *Ein Heldenleben* for each case. And there was "Alfred Hitchcock Presents" in which his hefty shadow appeared every week accompanied by Gounod's *Funeral March of a Marionette*.

I came to love this music as much or more than the programs they introduced and closed, though, at the time, I didn't even know the names of the pieces.

I came to love classical music the way I think everyone who loves classical gets to appreciate it—by hearing beautiful pieces over and over again until, finally, they want to hear more where those came from ... and they're hooked for the rest of their life.

Either that or they're hooked on Alfred Hitchcock and "The Shadow."

13
Buster and the Rats

If he had lived long enough Buster would have celebrated his 60th birthday this year. I still can't help thinking of him every time June 2nd rolls around. But while I was growing up, Buster was not the only animal sharing our home with us. We had rats in the basement at 89 Bluff Road. To my mother, who was never an animal lover, they were only slightly less welcome than Buster.

We tried everything we could think of to get rid of them, but the little rodents (some of them not so little) wouldn't go away.

My father and I set traps for them with imported cheddar cheese, but the rats would eat both the cheese and the traps without so much as cutting a toenail. I sprayed the walls and ceilings with rat-repellent gases. These caused some of them to move up to the first floor while the others stayed behind and coughed quietly.

Of course we called in the exterminators repeatedly. They fed the minibeasts some rather appetizing crystals which they called rat poison but which were evidently designed to speed up the rodents' multiplication and increase the pest-killers' business.

One of my most vivid childhood memories is the time I was walking through the dining room and I heard a scratching noise which sounded as though it was coming from behind the built-in radiator. I went to the kitchen,

Sixty Slices of Life... on Wry

took out the longest knife I could find, and stuck it in the narrow space between the radiator and the wall at the very spot where I thought I heard the noise.

Much to my surprise, the blade came up against something soft. I had only a split second to make a decision, which was to plunge in and pull back. A bleeding rat fell down the back of the radiator, came out the bottom, and proceeded to run as best it could. Petrified, I nevertheless chased the silently suffering rodent around the room, stabbing it again and again.

It was the largest, most disgusting rat I had ever met in person, so to speak. But still, upon reflection, I don't think he deserved the death penalty for no greater a crime than trying to warm himself next to our radiator. Nevertheless, after that no rat ever again dared to come up from the basement.

Buster was getting on in years when all this happened, and the older he got, the more flatulent he became. He eventually produced an odor which was so strong and disagreeable, the Soviet Union would have collapsed right then and there had we used the Buster bomb against them.

When Buster expelled gas, the noise would startle him, and he would turn around rapidly and look up at us with an innocent "Who-did-that?" expression. The smell was so strong, even Buster had to leave the room.

We, of course, tried everything we could think of to solve this problem as well. We bought an air spray, but the spray ganged up with the Bustergas to make the odor even more repulsive.

My mother purchased an electronic air purifier. It did nothing but distribute the stink equally to all parts of the room. She then tried changing Buster's dog food, figuring that what goes in eventually comes out (Newton's fourth law, I believe). And it did—more smelly than ever.

Sixty Slices of Life... on Wry

    We got some pills from the veterinarian. He promised they'd do the trick. But Buster stubbornly refused to take them, pretending he was a Christian Scientist.

    In desperation, we decided to keep poor old Buster outside. But the neighbors complained about air pollution and excessive noise from his continuous barking.

    That's when we put him in the basement.

    And we never saw another rat at 89 Bluff Road.

Sixty Slices of Life... on Wry

14
Inventing the Portable TV Camera

When I was about 12 years old I invented the world's first lightweight, portable, cableless, color TV camera. This was before anyone had color television, during the period when Edward R. Murrow's crew brought huge, heavy, black and white cameras with thick cables into the homes of the rich, the famous, and the powerful for his series, *Person to Person*.

Sony has not yet equalled the lightness and portability of the camera I developed. My instrument was as light as an empty Kleenex® box with an empty paper towel roll stuck through it. In fact it *was* an empty Kleenex® box with an empty paper towel roll stuck through it. My camera was solid state. It was beyond state-of-the-art. There were no wires, no tubes, no moving parts, no batteries, no electricity.

Yet the color resolution was perfect, the image completely lifelike and three-dimensional. I would be rich, famous, and powerful myself now except for a few minor problems:

First, I did not think of videotape, so all productions had to be live.

Second, I turned out to be the only person able to watch the programs I produced ("March of the Toy Soldiers," "The Buster Walk Jamboree," and "An Interview with Philip Flaxman, C.P.A.").

Sixty Slices of Life... on Wry

Third, the equipment wasn't waterproof, so it couldn't be used to cover outdoor events in inclement weather. At least not more than once.

In any case that camera gave me my first experience in television production, which turned out to be important to my later life.

So far, Kleenex®Vision is my one and only invention, my subsequent attempts at becoming a second Thomas Edison having been somewhat less successful.

15
The Kiss of Death

Multinational high tech corporations spend millions of dollars on market research before they come out with an important new product. How wasteful when all they need to do is to make a single telephone call—to me! And all they need to ask is one question: Will I buy their proposed product? If I answer, "Yes," they should know right then and there to drop the idea immediately. My endorsement of a new technology is the kiss of death for the product. I'll prove this beyond a shadow of a doubt with four real-life examples:

When I was 12, stereo records first came out on the market. I was sure they would fail to find buyers. After all, I reasoned (childishly, as it turned out), three dimensional depth is important in the visual sphere, but doesn't matter at all when it comes to sound. Who cares whether the trumpet is on the right or the left? High fidelity monaural sound was all we needed, thank you, so I didn't purchase a single stereo recording.

At about the same time a new camera was introduced to the market. It was called the Stereo Realist. It took double slides, each separated from the other by the same distance as our eyes. You viewed these slides with a battery-powered device through which your left eye would see the left slide and your right eye would see the right slide. A flashlight-sized light bulb would illuminate both slides. The resulting

Sixty Slices of Life... on Wry

full-color image appeared to be truly three-dimensional.

You could also view these slides with a projector, but then you had to wear special glasses to achieve the three-dimensional effect.

I begged for and received a Stereo Realist camera for my 13th birthday. After all, I reasoned, stereo was as important to vision as it was unimportant to sound. I still think I was correct, but I have to explain to people today what a Stereo Realist is—or was—and you'd have a hard time finding these cameras now. Even I don't own one any more. I still have several years' worth of stereo slides which no one ever looks at, and a viewer which is gathering dust.

At age 13, I purchased a reel-to-reel audio tape recorder. When, a few years later, cassette players were introduced to the market, I ignored them and stuck with my big, cumbersome reel-to-reel equipment. After all, no one claimed that the little cassettes sounded as good as the big reels, and who needed a portable tape recorder anyway?

Well, I still have one of those big reels filled with recordings of myself and my brothers playing the piano as well as of the heated discussion between my parents on the most important topic of the day: the fat on the lamb chops my mother served for dinner. But I got rid of the tape recorder so many years ago I can't remember how I disposed of it. To find one today you would have to go past the Edsel in a cemetery for departed technology.

And no, I didn't buy an Edsel, so you can't blame that one on me!

But I was the first on my block to own a Betamax videocassette recorder. VHS machines were available, too, but their picture quality wasn't as good and the Beta videocassettes were smaller.

I still have my Beta, along with a bunch of Beta cassettes I never play. But I was forced to purchase a VHS ma-

Sixty Slices of Life... on Wry

chine if I wanted to view any cassettes from a video rental store. That is before DVDs and Netflix came on the scene. So now I have all those videocassettes that no one ever watches taking up shelf space. In any case, the moment I purchased a Beta VCR, Sony should have known to discontinue the product, at least in the U.S.

Now, if it weren't for the iPod, Apple Computers would be in serious trouble. They went wrong from the moment I purchased a Mac Plus rather than an IBM personal computer, though they didn't know it. They saved themselves only by developing the iPod, which succeeded, of course, because I didn't buy one. When I retired from full-time work in public broadcasting, I was given an iPod as a thank-God-we-don't-have-to-put-up-with-you-anymore departure gift. Not being able to find any use for it, I gave it to my teenage granddaughter. It has been sticking to her ears ever since, and Apple's success continued with the iPhone, because I didn't buy that either.

I went with Macintosh originally because it was a much better, more user-friendly, system. Mac is still superior to IBM and its clones, though Windows software has certainly narrowed the gap. But if there is anything I have learned in my experience buying high-tech equipment, it is that Americans will go for the inferior product every time, as long as it is cheaper.

I now have an iMac, which I spend more time with every day than I do with my wife. But I'm afraid if I upgrade to the newest version, the company may yet go under.

Perhaps I should write to the CEO of Apple Computers and offer—for a reasonable sum of, let's say, $1,000,000—to replace my iMac with a computer that uses a Windows operating system. That could solve my financial problems and secure Apple's success simultaneously.

16
Sink or Swim

In May, 1958, I was winding up my sixth and final year at the Horace Mann School for Boys. Horace Mann, the man, was one of the founders of our nation's public school system. But Horace Mann, the school, was, and is, a very exclusive, private institution located in the posh Riverdale section of the Bronx, New York.

I was not a happy camper at H.M. The older I got, the less pleased I was with its all-male environment. I was elected president of my class for four out of the six years, running on a platform favoring the admission of female students. And that happened in time, but not in time to do me any good.

H. M. was tough not only academically, but physically. Their motto was "strong mind, strong body." All students were to be "well-rounded," whether they wanted to be or not. And, in order to graduate, they needed to pass a number of athletic, as well as academic, tests.

As poor a student as I was, I was an even worse athlete. My lack of strength was exceeded only by my lack of coordination, and my lack of ability was surpassed only by my lack of interest. But somehow I managed to pass the push-up and the sit-up tests, and even learned to do what may be charitably described as a semi-somersault. There was one physical exam, though, which I dreaded above all others, and it was all that stood between me and my high

Sixty Slices of Life... on Wry

school diploma—the swim survival test.

I stayed up nights trying to think of ways to avoid it—but nobody escaped Mr. Malthaner's survival test. Malthaner, after all, was an ex-Marine type: short, stocky, muscular, and mean. His tolerance for deviation from the norm was as long as his crew-cut hair. His discipline was as tight as the skin on his smileless face. In his book there was no such thing as the exception which proved the rule. The rule was the rule and should be followed to its smallest letter. He would have made a perfect drill sergeant during World War II. But World War II had been over for 13 years, whether he realized it or not, and we—the flabby, intellectual high school students of Horace Mann—were his only canon fodder.

When the fatal day arrived, I was the one student to wish that the school didn't have an indoor swimming pool. The others regarded it as a blessing second only to air conditioning on those hot and humid days at the end of the term.

I felt thankful then for only one thing—that the inventor of the alphabet had decided to put "A", "B", "C", "D" and "E" all before the letter "F." The test was administered in alphabetical order, in small groups, with each boy leaving the pool area when his turn was up.

On that terrible day I would have gladly changed names with Bernie Zucker. Barring that remote possibility, many members of the class would still be standing around with nothing better to do than to watch my agony as they waited their turn.

As I said, Horace Mann was an all-boys school, and—perhaps due to its Greek philosophy of education, perhaps due to some other, less enlightened reason—bathing suits were not allowed in the pool. I was very embarrassed about

Sixty Slices of Life... on Wry

displaying my unclothed body in public, because I was slower to mature than other boys my age and didn't like to facilitate comparisons.

So, at the start of the swim survival test, the entire class of about 90 was lined up stark naked on both sides of the pool. At the risk of looking formal, I placed my towel around my waist and waited nervously for my name to be called.

Malthaner shouted the names of the first group of boys, his deep, masculine, athletic voice bouncing between the four walls of the tiled room.

Arenberg and the others jumped in and the rest of the class watched as they swam back and forth across the pool four times lengthwise. They stopped short of the wall of the deep end and proceeded to bob up and down in the water for the prescribed ten minutes. The sound of Malthaner's whistle shrilled through the room and the students emerged, smiling and self-satisfied, from the pool. The next group jumped in and repeated the same routine.

By the time they were finishing up, I was carefully biting the skin from around my fingernails. Most of the students who took the test left the room with short, rapid breaths; many of those who remained scratched their dandruff or picked their pimples with ever-increasing anxiety. But no one seemed as terrorized as I was. Despite the hot, humid air, my teeth were chattering and my legs were shaking with fright.

If only someone—just one single solitary student—would fail the test first. I so dreaded being the only one! I believed that, with an extraordinary effort, I could probably swim the four lengths, but I was sure that that would completely exhaust me. I knew I could never remain there bobbing up and down in water over my head for ten minutes.

I thought of going up to Malthaner right then and tell-

Sixty Slices of Life... on Wry

ing him that I just couldn't do it. That would save everyone's time—and my embarrassment. Surely they wouldn't refuse me my diploma after six years of hard academic work simply because I didn't stay in some silly water for ten minutes. Would they?

Yes they would, Malthaner assured me as he sent me back to the line. "And take that towel off 'til ya need it, Flaxman. We know what ya look like!"

I had only a few more minutes to, somehow, get out of there. If the water had had a high voltage electric current running through it I couldn't have been any more scared of going in. I racked my brains for a way to leave, honorably or dishonorably, and was just about to run for the shower room exit when I heard my group called.

Some 70 students watched as I reluctantly removed my towel and jumped into the pool with the others. I swam its length back and fourth four times, more slowly than the others, becoming tired by the third lap and exhausted on the fourth. But I finished these rounds and remained out in the deep water treading despite my fatigue.

"Bob, don't tread!" Malthaner shouted.

I pretended not to hear. I couldn't see much point in bobbing up and down when I hardly had the strength to just tread there with my head above the water line. I started floating on my back.

"Bob, damn you, or you'll stay in that water all day!"

But I had had enough. I had to rest even if it meant repeating the whole test some other day. I just wasn't in shape for this and I knew it. Maybe if I practiced bobbing for a few days, staying in longer each time, I could pass the test. Yes, that's what I should do, I told myself. Why hadn't I thought of that sooner? I swam over to the pool wall and placed my

Sixty Slices of Life... on Wry

hand on it, starting to raise myself out of the water.

"Bob, damn you!" Malthaner shouted and his foot slammed down on my hand. I slid back into the pool, full of pain, hatred, and water. I used my remaining strength to swim over to the other side where I planned to climb out. Malthaner ran around the edge of the pool and was waiting for me when I got there.

"The sooner you start bobbing, the sooner you'll get out!" Malthaner yelled. I heard the words reflected from every tile and a new sense of fear overcame me. Could Malthaner keep me in here against my will? That possibility had never occurred to me before. I thought that all I had to do was to give up and I could get out if I were willing to forfeit the precious H.M. diploma. But it seemed that Malthaner wouldn't accept defeat as an answer. And I felt helpless against him.

Then I got an idea. I started swimming, as rapidly as I could, for the shallow part of the pool. At least I would be able to stand there—even if for only a second!

But no sooner had I started in that direction than Malthaner jumped into the pool ahead of me. He angrily grabbed me and threw me back into the deeper area. Choking with water, I swam back toward Malthaner hoping to hold onto him for just a moment's rest. But Malthaner's large, iron hand pushed me by the face back into the ever-present liquid.

By this time the other students had done their required bobbing and, with Malthaner's permission, had left the pool. I remained behind, swimming first in one direction and then another, using what little energy I had left in desperate attempts to escape my tormentor. But Malthaner was much quicker and much stronger and I soon learned that my attempts would all be in vain.

Sixty Slices of Life... on Wry

I then started treading water again. Malthaner stayed in the pool by my side. I had no way of knowing it at the time, but I had been in the water for 15 minutes.

"The sooner you start bobbing, the sooner you'll get out!" Malthaner yelled again. The walls repeated the message.

I felt for sure that I would drown any second and by this time I didn't care. At least that way I could rest. And it would serve Malthaner right.

I stopped treading water. My head stayed beneath the surface for a few seconds until I felt a desperate need for air. I raised my mouth above the water, took a deep breath, and fell back exhausted under the water once again. I did this a second time. And then again. Suddenly I realized that I was bobbing! Next time up for air I yelled out to Malthaner that I had bobbed and demanded to be allowed to leave the pool.

"I've been in more than ten minutes!" I shouted. I had been in a good half-hour, or, at least, it seemed that way to me.

But Malthaner ignored me. I resorted to begging.

"Please let me out. Please!" I cried, only vaguely concerned at this point with my humiliation. Malthaner told me to shut up and keep bobbing.

"The sooner you start bobbing, the sooner you'll get out," he said. And this time I believed him.

When I had been in the pool for what seemed like hours, I felt delirious but, strangely enough, almost rested. I could go on like this all day, I thought, and I no longer expected Malthaner to ever let me out.

When the swimming instructor finally did speak, I was startled by the break of silence. The news that I could come out had to be repeated before I realized that I wasn't hallucinating.

Sixty Slices of Life... on Wry

The fact that I had passed my swim survival test surprised me at first, then pleased me greatly when I climbed out of the pool and discovered what I had accomplished. I had been in there for almost an hour without a single moment's rest while the rest of the class waited impatiently for their turns.

• • • •

On graduation day, the Class of '58 stood in line together for the last time, on this occasion fully dressed in ties and jackets with carnations in our lapels. Once again we were in alphabetical order. But now it was to accept our diplomas.

Tears came to my eyes as Dr. Mitchell Gratwick, the headmaster, handed me mine. But it wasn't because I was emotionally moved by the experience or sorry to leave H.M. after all those difficult years.

It was because I was allergic to carnations.

• • • •

Now, writing on the 50th anniversary of my high school graduation, I realize that my life itself has turned out to be one big swim survival test. It hasn't been as difficult to pass as I feared it would be, but I had to let my head go under once in a while, to sink temporarily in order to rebound later, to relax and go with the flow, to make the best of whatever troubled waters I found myself in... and, above all, to try not to make too many waves.

Michigan

17
Coke Caps & Classics

In 1958 the University of Michigan in Ann Arbor found me attempting to pursue my B.A. degree. During the second semester I shared a dormitory room with a classical music enthusiast from Ohio named ... well, I had better not divulge his name for fear of incriminating the guilty.

Alan, I'll call him, was a short, quiet young man with eyeglasses and a completely pockmarked face. In the semester I spent rooming with him, I never once heard him raise his voice.

In fact, it became rather a challenge for me to try to get his goat. One evening he wanted to turn out the light promptly at 10 p.m. and go to sleep. I wanted to continue reading my Modern Library book. I was hooked on these small, hardcover editions at the time and read one after another rather than anything that was assigned in class.

Alan turned off the ceiling light from the switch near the door and went to bed.

I turned the light back on and resumed my reading.

Alan got up and turned the switch back off.

I got up and turned the light back on.

Alan walked calmly over to my reading chair and, without saying a word, grabbed my book and broke it in two over his raised knee. Then he quietly walked back to the light switch, turned it off, and went to bed.

Sixty Slices of Life... on Wry

• • • •

Ordinarily Alan and I got along quite well, though he was a year ahead of me and we didn't do very much together. He asked me, nevertheless, to accompany him many nights at two or three o'clock in the morning as he made the rounds of all the dormitory rec rooms, emptying the soda machines of their bottle caps before the cleanup crews arrived.

I had to bite my tongue to keep from laughing as this dignified, potential future professor of linguistics surreptitiously stuck his hand in the bottle-cap catcher and pulled out the caps from one machine after another.

Sometimes there were still students up at that time, watching television or cramming for an exam. Alan would wait a while for them to leave, but then, tired and impatient, sneak up to the soda machine and try to pull out the caps unnoticed.

Back in our room Alan would go through all the caps, separating the Coke caps from the rest, which he threw right out in the wastebasket. The Coke caps were all boxed and sent to his mother in Cleveland where the high school which brought in the most Coke bottle tops to the local A&P supermarket would win a $2,000 prize. Alan wanted to make sure his high school was victorious.

But the janitor who emptied Alan's wastebasket never knew that.

• • • •

Alan was so in love with classical music that he could enjoy a superb recorded performance regardless of the sound quality. He particularly admired the great opera voices of the past, and would listen to these on 78 r.p.m. recordings which were so full of scratches and ticks that I myself couldn't hear

Sixty Slices of Life... on Wry

the music for the noise.

The U. of M. library still had a number of these old records back then. I'm sure they don't anymore because most—if not all—of them were undoubtedly found missing sometime after Alan graduated. You see, my dear roommate "borrowed" these records without ever checking them out ... or returning them, for that matter.

Rain or shine, he wore an oversized trench coat every time he went to the library. Afterwards he rationalized that no one else appreciated these recordings, and the library was switching to LPs anyway.

I wonder what university—or penitentiary—Alan is in now.

18
Getting High with Eleanor

There are so many people on the face of the earth it is sometimes hard to believe that each one is unique. Some surely are more special than others. There was only one George Gershwin, for example, only one Alfred Hitchcock, only one Mark Twain, only one Eleanor Roosevelt.

I have learned—the hard way—not to miss the rare opportunities that present themselves to get to know such true individuals at least a little bit better.

One of my most important lessons took place in 1960 when my friend, Marc Alan Zagoren, and I were returning to the University of Michigan in Ann Arbor from our New Jersey homes after Thanksgiving break.

We were waiting in Newark Airport for our bargain-basement night coach to begin boarding, discussing, as it happened, *Sunrise at Campobello*, the motion picture biography of Franklin and Eleanor Roosevelt.

Just then, an airline official escorted an elderly lady past the entire line of travelers. I recognized her immediately, not only from all the photographs I had seen of her in newspapers and magazines, but because I had worked with her on a U. of M. educational TV program two years earlier. She was Eleanor Roosevelt.

Mrs. Roosevelt was brought through the ground-floor gate directly onto the tarmac, and, although I was at the very head of the line, I couldn't see which plane she was heading towards as the door was closed right behind her.

When, a few minutes later, the regular passengers were permitted to board, I was the first one on the plane, Marc following just behind. As soon as I entered the cabin, I glanced over all the seats to see if Mrs. Roosevelt had boarded our plane. I saw no one.

Kiddingly, for Marc's entertainment, I started looking under the seats, calling out, none too softly, in an exaggerated, high-pitched tone of voice, "Eleanor, Eleanor, where are you Eleanor?"

I looked up and, much to my surprise, saw Mrs. Roosevelt slouched down in the window seat nearest to my suddenly red-faced head. She had been sleeping, but her eyes opened and I thought this deeply compassionate woman looked at me as though I might be the one and only exception to her opposition to the death penalty.

"Oh, Mrs. Roosevelt!" I blurted out, "I'm so sorry that I woke you! Please forgive me!"

Without a word of either forgiveness or recrimination, she fell back asleep and I prayed that somehow she hadn't heard my "Eleanors," or that perhaps she would think she had had a strange nightmare.

Had I not made such a fool of myself, I would have sat in the empty seat right next to Mrs. Roosevelt, even though there were many other choices. Instead, I sat just across the aisle, with Marc on my other side, wondering what a former First Lady, an ambassador to the United Nations, a woman of aristocratic upbringing and distinction, was doing by herself on a middle-of-the-night flight from Newark to Detroit, in close proximity to two silly college students.

I was curious to see if the great lady snored, but fell asleep before I could find out.

When we arrived at our destination I dared to speak

Sixty Slices of Life... on Wry

to her as if nothing had happened, reminding her of our work together on the TV program. She was the host; I was the microphone boom operator, so it wasn't too surprising that she didn't quite remember me.

Mrs. Roosevelt asked me to repeat everything I said into her other ear as she was deaf in the one closest to me—and to the aisle. I felt relieved. Maybe she hadn't heard a thing and hadn't wished the death penalty on me, after all.

I asked Mrs. Roosevelt if she were going to speak in Detroit, and she replied that she was headed for a talk in Port Huron. That was about the extent of our conversation as reported in a long letter I wrote later the same day. With collegiate humor typical of the times, and, perhaps, of all times, I joked that I had slept with Eleanor Roosevelt.

My correspondent might have had a good laugh. But I had had a brief opportunity to talk alone with the First Lady of the World—and I muffed it.

19
Room for Rent; Will Accept Whites

I had a real problem finding housing for my last semester at the University of Michigan. I couldn't locate a landlord willing to sign less than a nine-month lease. Finally I resorted to a real estate agent who specialized in apartment rentals.

He drove me around and around town, but the search for a one-semester lease appeared fruitless.

In 1961 Ann Arbor was still a very segregated town and the agent asked me if I would consider an apartment in the Negro section. I said I wouldn't mind at all and he drove me to a three-floor boarding house which had a sign in front which read: "ROOM FOR RENT. WILL ACCEPT WHITES."

I rented the room on the second floor. Everyone else in the building was black. In fact the old three-story frame house seemed to be a microcosm of black society. An uneducated janitor, his wife and 18-year-old daughter lived on the ground floor. University students occupied the rooms on my floor. A part-time bible salesman from Detroit lived at the end of the hall. The third floor was inhabited by an unemployed alcoholic and I don't remember who else.

What I do remember is how that 18-year-old daughter on the ground floor looked at me the first time she saw me, and every time she saw me after that. No woman had ever stared at me before (or, I confess, since) with that much

Sixty Slices of Life... on Wry

desire in her eyes. At first I thought it was just because she was so unused to seeing whites in the neighborhood. But, as it turned out, she was giving me the eye for a more basic reason.

She was my opposite in more than skin color and social class. Where my face was plain and pimply, hers was beautiful and smooth. Where my chest was flat and unnoticeable, hers was pronounced and impossible to ignore. Where her belly was flat and unnoticeable, mine protruded into a small pot. Where I led a life of the mind, she appeared to have more athletic interests.

After about a month in that rooming house, I decided to give a party in my large room and invite everyone in the building. Attendance was good, and it included the girl with the I-want-your-bod-now deep brown eyes. People drank, they talked, they seemed to have a good time. And, eventually, they left... except for her.

Alone together for the first time, she said to me: "You know, I have a crush on someone in this building."

"You do?" I replied, acting innocently. "Who is it?"

"Guess," she said.

I went through the men in the building, one by one, and, except for her and her mother, everyone was male.

"Was it Sammy?"

"No."

"Was it Ojo?"

"No."

Finally there was no one else to name but myself. By that time I had joined her on the floor where she had been sitting all during the party.

I bent over and kissed her on the mouth. She opened her mouth right away and our tongues met. My right hand went feeling that wonderfully opposite part of her upper

Sixty Slices of Life... on Wry

anatomy. When she did nothing to stop me, my hand went down to another opposite anatomical area, one which I somehow neglected to mention in my list of attracting opposites above.

I very nearly lost my virginity that day but, as they say, almost doesn't count. When the two of us ended up in my bed with no clothes on and me on top of her, I didn't know exactly, precisely where to put ... it ... and I was petrified that I would put it in the wrong place. She, for her part, just laid there passively enjoying my caresses. She didn't touch my you-know-what, never mind place it where it wanted to go. So nothing happened of any consequence, fortunately for both of our unprotected futures, and she left shortly afterwards, feeling, I think, that I had rejected her.

I tried several times to date her after that, but she would have nothing more to do with me, and never gave me that look of hers again.

I left the U. of M. in February 1962 with a B.A. degree and a certificate in journalism. I had met the university's graduation requirements by taking such courses as philosophy, botany, and French. But what I needed to meet *my* graduation requirements was a basic course in human anatomy.

France

20
Incident of Anti-Semitism

After graduating from college in 3½ years, I convinced my father to let me spend a semester studying French language and culture at the Sorbonne in Paris. The truth was that I wanted to study French women, but I couldn't tell him that and expect him to pay my way.

While in Paris I lived in an area of student dormitories on the outskirts of the city called the Cité Universitaire. I was sitting in the bar of my dorm, the Fondation des Etats-Unis, when one of three girls at the next table asked me if I had a light. I didn't smoke but was still altruistic enough to carry matches for just such an occasion.

Two of the girls were sisters from Portugal—the other was from Peru. I chatted with them a while when a young Arab-looking man came up to them, said, "Bonsoir," and joined them. He was immediately introduced to me. His name, Adil. His nationality, Turkish.

"What was your name?" he asked me as if he didn't quite catch it the first time around.

"Fred," I answered, rolling the "r" à la française.

"I mean your last name," he insisted.

I know that Turkey isn't an Arab country and that it isn't known for anti-Semitism. But I could just read this Turk's mind, he was thinking so intensely: *You are a Jew, aren't you! Tell me your last name so I can be sure—so I can be sure you are my enemy.*

Sixty Slices of Life... on Wry

"Flaxman," I answered, retaining the French accent half out of habit, half out of fear.

"You are Jewish, aren't you?" he said in very good English.

"Yes," I replied. The "yes" was emphatic. It was designed to say also *and I am not ashamed*, but I don't think that quite came across.

"May I explain something to you?" I asked politely, after a very embarrassing pause.

"Certainly," Adil replied.

"I don't mind telling you my ethnic background," I lied, "but it just isn't very tactful to ask someone such a personal question outright like that when you've just met."

"I know," he said kindly. "I'm terribly sorry, but you look somewhat Jewish and I wondered whether or not you were. Being Jewish myself, I am very interested."

Sixty Slices of Life... on Wry

21
France Was Years Ahead

When I first went to France as a student in 1962, I thought it was a charming, picturesque country—but a bit backward. It now appears, though, that the French were a quarter century ahead of us—at least concerning ecology, a word most Americans (and most French) had never heard of.

Instead of blowing their noses in paper tissues, the French used cloth handkerchiefs—a word that has almost disappeared from English. You can use handkerchiefs over and over, of course, throwing them in the washing machine with all the other dirty clothes. Buying box after box of disposable tissues really adds up compared to the one-time cost of a handkerchief. Soft cloth is more comfortable on a sore nose and more resistant to tears. But despite all these advantages, I had to return to France to find a store which sold real hankies when I decided that Kimberly-Clark took too much of my family's budget.

Much to my horror, toilet paper was almost unknown in France in 1962. The little to be found—in hotels too expensive to be frequented by students—consisted of tiny individual sheets of coarse crepe paper. The hotels I could afford used recycled newspaper. Newspapers were also the principal means for wrapping fish in fish markets. And the French also found a use for old newspapers that many present-day Americans would find highly unusual

Sixty Slices of Life... on Wry

and perhaps unhealthy: they read them.

When I went shopping, I had to remember to bring my own bag. French stores never supplied them, either out of paper or plastic. French housewives all had their "filets"—string nets that took practically no room at all in their handbags and yet miraculously opened up to fit everything they needed for the day.

To an American accustomed to shopping for food once a week and living out of the freezer the rest of the time, the practice of shopping daily seemed like a waste of time and energy. But I had to admit that the fresh meats, fruits, and vegetables were much better than the frozen kinds. And, it turns out, much healthier.

What bugged me most about the inexpensive French hotels I stayed in at the time was their chintzy use of electricity. The lights in the halls would stay on for about a minute and then go off automatically—usually when you were halfway down a flight of stairs trying to make your way in the middle of the night to the closest bathroom, after having consumed a bit too much cheap French wine. When you finally got there, the light in the "W.C." would go on only when you turned the lock on the door—if you could ever find it in the dark. The light would turn off again automatically when you unlocked the door.

Many people must have lost their lives falling down stairs or tripping over things in the suddenly darkened halls, but this system sure saved electricity—and the importation of oil as well. The French conserved energy long before Americans knew what the term meant.

In 1962 there were only two black and white channels available on French television—and both were public stations. The programs were mostly educational documentaries or round-table discussions. There were no commercials.

Sixty Slices of Life... on Wry

As a result, French people didn't watch much TV and when they did they had a better than 50-50 chance of learning something from what they saw.

At the same time, Americans in large cities had a choice of seven channels. They could watch cultural programs such as "I Love Lucy" and documentaries like "Candid Camera." PBS didn't exist and there was no such thing as "Sesame Street." American kids were glued to cartoons and commercials, while French children were outside getting exercise and fresh air.

Back then, very few French people could afford to have their own cars. Almost everyone used public transportation. The Paris subway was crowded during rush hours. Trains going all over the country were packed at the end of the week and the beginning of holiday or vacation periods.

Today France operates the fastest, most modern trains in the world, while our highways become more and more congested. A few years ago Californians passed a bond measure designed to lead to what we call high-speed trains —125 miles per hour. The opposition claimed that Americans would no longer take trains—even quick, modern, clean, comfortable ones. The French trains carry passengers at 186 miles per hour, and seats are by reservation only.

As far ahead of us as the French were in ecological conservation in 1962, we have nearly caught up with them today. It's not that we've learned to turn off lights that weren't needed or that we've developed solar soda can disposals. It's just that they've become more like us.

When I stayed at my French sister-in-law's house near Roanne a few years ago, I noticed she had a box of paper tissues in each bathroom, disposable napkins were

Sixty Slices of Life... on Wry

used at each meal, pure mountain stream water came in plastic bottles, she had a freezer so large it had to be kept in a separate building, and the lights in her house stayed on until they were turned off manually.

I guess if you want to visit an ecologically advanced nation nowadays, you have to go to Afghanistan or Tibet.

22
Love Par Avion

I could never picture myself in the military. My freedom was always so important to me, I could not conceive of giving it up to blindly follow orders, never mind actually going to war. How could I shoot a total stranger, someone who had never done me any harm, someone whom I might even like if I got to know him, when I was incapable of crushing an insect without remorse? So, when I graduated from the University of Michigan a semester early in January, 1962, I decided to stay in school and continue my student deferment rather than face the possibility of being drafted.

I applied to the Sorbonne in Paris where they had a special program to teach French language, literature, and culture to foreigners. Although I was really more interested in French wine, women, and song, I was accepted, and I flew to France from New York via Luxembourg on Icelandic Airlines within a month of earning my B.A.

At the Foundation des Etats-Unis (the U.S. House) at the Cité Universitaire, I was paired with a roommate. Although he was French, he showed up only at bedtime—or not at all—so he wasn't much help in terms of practicing my French. Most of the others in the U.S. House were American. At the Sorbonne itself, although the lectures were in French, the students in this special program were from all over the world.

Sixty Slices of Life... on Wry

I thus met Americans everyplace, or other foreign students who spoke English and were happy to practice it on me. I was spending 24 hours a day in the capital of France, and hadn't advanced beyond elementary restaurant French. I could ask, "Combien est-ce?" (How much is this?), with an accent that made the waiter cringe, but couldn't understand the quickly-rattled-off "Deux francs quatre-vingt quatorze" (2,94 F) reply.

In the lobby of the Foundation des Etats-Unis there was a large bulletin board. It was divided into sections for students seeking traveling partners, roommates, apartments, used cars, or furniture, etc. One section was devoted to English speakers who wanted to practice their French with French speakers and vice versa. I was looking at that section one day when I found this notice:

I wish to exchange French-English conversations with someone who also enjoys reading and music. Please write me at (address), Fontenay-aux-Roses.

A. STORY

I couldn't figure out from reading this whether the person who placed it was French or American. The last name, after all, was very English. I also wondered whether it was placed there by a boy or a girl, since "A" was not very revealing. But I knew that, whoever it was, he or she had the same interests I had, and I decided to write.

That was more easily decided than done, since my French writing ability was even worse than my speaking skills. I had met a young Frenchman from Corsica, Charles

Sixty Slices of Life… on Wry

Arnaud, who lived in a nearby dorm and who was very friendly and kind. I asked him for his help.

In the end, the letter I sent to A. Story was far more Charles' wording than mine. I didn't realize it then, but his French was particularly old-fashioned and flowery—the complete opposite of what would have been required to reflect my informal American personality.

But A. Story replied. "A" turned out to be for "Annick," who was French, although her father was an Englishman born in Paris.

It was a while before we actually met, since I went off to Spain for spring break with a couple of American friends. When we finally did see each other for the first time it was at the Fondation, where Annick picked me up to go to our first concert together.

As this was a totally blind date, without even a mutual friend to introduce us, I was very pleasantly surprised by how attractive she was. Annick was tall for a French person, slender, with straight red hair, freckles, sparkling green eyes, and a thin little nose. Her English turned out to be good enough to be employed as Helena Rubinstein's bilingual secretary!

Although I was 22, I felt immediately like a boy compared to this young French woman, whose maturity made me think that she was several years my senior. She seemed so dignified, refined, reserved, yet self-confident.

We started talking in English, then switched to French during the intermission of the concert we attended, and stuck to French when the event was over. This is a pattern we repeated at each of the five or six concerts we went to together. From the first, though, the disparity in our language abilities was obvious: she was trying to perfect her skills; I was trying to make myself understood.

Sixty Slices of Life... on Wry

Annick was an excellent teacher—kind, understanding, patient, uncritical. Her pronunciation of French was clear, slow, and deliberate. I felt that she was helping me a great deal more than I was helping her, and I was grateful to her for it.

At our first meeting, Annick made it clear to me that there had been a previous response to her bulletin board notice from a young man who was interested in more than just improving his French. He wanted to practice certain other, more basic skills. That was why she had put up another card, this time concealing her gender. That veiled warning, combined with the gap in our language abilities and, I thought, ages, created a teacher-student relationship between us that never got very personal.

During the intermission of the last concert we went to before I was to leave for Scandinavia for the summer, Annick asked me if I would recommend some books by American authors which she would enjoy reading and would help her improve her English.

"Instead of trying to think of the right books now off the top of my head," I answered, "why don't I wait until I get back to the U.S. in September and look at the list I keep of all the books I have read. Then I'll send you my recommendations."

"You keep a list of all the books you've read?" she asked.

"Yes," I reiterated, thinking it was probably a compulsively orderly thing to do.

"So do I!" she exclaimed. Neither of us had ever met anyone who did this before.

When I got back to the States I remembered my promise. I sent Annick a long thank-you letter, in the best French I could muster for the occasion, and enclosed the lists

Sixty Slices of Life... on Wry

of recommended books. I even added a list of my favorite classical music. I thought this was the least I could do after all she had done for me. I didn't expect a reply.

But Annick sent me a long letter in return, thanking me for the two lists. Hers was such a nice, friendly letter, I simply could not let it go unanswered. Anyway, it was good for my French.

And thus started a correspondence between two people who enjoyed writing as much as reading and music. I tried to discuss philosophy and world events in my letters, frustrated by a totally inadequate French vocabulary which limited me to the words of a retarded provincial elementary school student.

Nevertheless, as the months went by, the letters got more personal. At one point I broached the subject of religion, not having any idea what Annick's views were on the subject. I didn't know whether she was a Catholic, like most French people, especially from Brittany, or whether she was a Protestant of some sort, since her father was English. She could even have been Jewish, for all I knew, although she certainly would have broken all the stereotypes at once if she had been.

When I confessed that I was a Jewish agnostic who felt that all religions were a bunch of lies, I thought my letter might terminate our increasingly warmer correspondence. But it didn't. On the contrary, I learned that not only did Annick subscribe to the same views, she came from a family that was anti-religious too. In fact, anti-clericalism was handed down from generation to generation on her father's side the way religion is in many families. Since her grandfather and great-grandfather were journalists and authors, their unconventional sentiments can still be seen in the published writings they left behind.

Sixty Slices of Life... on Wry

The more we wrote back and forth, the more it seemed as though Annick and I shared the same tastes, philosophies, attitudes and interests. By Christmas, when I sent her a copy of Mahler's *First Symphony* and another recording I could hardly afford, I started to wonder whether Annick was "Miss It" or just a very good letter writer. By Easter I felt I had to get back to France to find out.

Getting back to France less than a year after the conclusion of my first visit was a bit of a challenge. My father had paid for my first trip as part of my education. He certainly would not fund a return visit for the purposes I had in mind. Clearly this trip also had to be necessary for my education if he were to be convinced to pay for it.

To get my M.A. from Stanford—where I was then keeping out of the military by studying political science and international relations—I had to take three quarters worth of seminars, write various term papers and compose a thesis. For my thesis topic I selected *Civil Liberties Under the French Fifth Republic* because nothing was available on the subject outside of France. My advisor agreed to this subject without a problem. After all, he didn't have to foot my bill to do research in Paris. Getting my father to go along was more difficult.

"Why couldn't you do your thesis on *Civil Liberties Under the Kennedy Administration?*" he asked.

"I'm sorry, Dad," I explained, "but I can't write about American government. I'm specializing in international relations, specifically France and Sweden, and my thesis topic has already been approved. Anyway, I don't think it would be any cheaper to go to Sweden."

My father reluctantly gave the trip his OK, and tickets were purchased for me on the S.S. France—not exactly the typical student's method of crossing the Atlantic.

Sixty Slices of Life... on Wry

But the night before my scheduled departure, I nearly blew the whole thing. It occurred to me that I should mention something about Annick to my parents. After all, they didn't know that she existed, and I didn't want them to be totally surprised if my relationship developed into ... well, something serious.

My father was a certified public accountant and he could add two and two faster than an electronic calculator. He was ready to call off the trip the moment he heard that there was a French girl over there who interested me. But my father was, above all, a practical man. The boat left the next day. The tickets were paid for and it was too late for a refund.

So I left for France from New York on June 13, 1963. During the five days of luxurious dining and entertainment, I wondered what I should do when I first saw Annick, who was planning to meet me on arrival. After all, our letters had been getting warmer and warmer.

Would I even recognize her after the nine months which had gone by without seeing her? Should I kiss her, European style, once on each cheek, accompanied by a mild hug? Should I kiss her on the lips? Should I kiss her more passionately while giving her a tight hug?

On June 18, 1963—a date we have celebrated ever since as the Anniversary of the Great Landing— the S.S. France pulled into the port of Cherbourg. Annick was waiting in the crowd on the quai, smiling broadly and waving her hand at me. I recognized her instantly. I disembarked as soon as I could, we ran to each other as in a scene from a romantic French movie, and I hugged her, kissed her on both cheeks and hugged her again.

The passionate kisses were to come just a few days later when I learned that Annick was not just a very good

Sixty Slices of Life... on Wry

letter writer. She did turn out to be "an older woman"—but only by a year.

• • • •

It was time to meet Annick's parents. She called home to Dinard and told them about me, and we planned a weekend trip there by train. Her mother, being French, wanted to know right away not about my financial situation, job prospects or religious beliefs, but about my eating habits.

"What does he drink with his meals?" she asked, trying to prepare a dinner that would please this visitor from another continent and culture.

"Milk," Annick replied matter-of-factly.

"Du lait!" her mother exclaimed in total surprise. "But that's not healthy!"

She turned out to be right on this subject, as on just about anything else that had to do with food.

• • • •

The French are very protective of their women, or, at least, those who are foolish enough to want to marry nationals of other countries. They make *l'étranger* (their word for "foreigner" is the same as for "stranger") go through all kinds of loops before they'll grant a marriage license. Or, at least, that's the way it was back then.

With so complicated a procedure, it was virtually impossible to accomplish it without a lawyer. So I engaged one, and he supplied me with a check list of documents I had to furnish, statements I had to have notarized, and people whose permission I had to obtain! I don't think I had to prove that I loved Annick, but I sure had to demonstrate that I could support her! And I had to collect testaments

Sixty Slices of Life… on Wry

to my good character. Of course any morally suspect, alcoholic Frenchman could marry a French woman with no problem.

The wedding itself was a civil ceremony which took place at the Town Hall of Dinard. Having never been married before, and not understanding French all that well, my only clue as to what would happen was my vague recollection of the wedding scenes in a bunch of old Hollywood movies.

So I sat there waiting for the French equivalent of:

"Do you, Fred Flaxman, take Annick Story as your lawful, wedded wife, to hold and to honor, in good times and bad, in sickness and in health, for the rest of your life?"

But those lines never came. Instead the deputy mayor read from the civil law on the subject of marriage. There came a time though when I was supposed to say, "Oui," but I didn't, because I didn't know what was going on.

My future mother-in-law, sitting just behind me, must have been close to having a heart attack when she jabbed me in the back and whispered to me, "Say, '*Oui*'!"

I did, and we were married on September 10, the very day that President Kennedy issued an executive order exempting married men from the draft. By the time President Johnson was drafting married men to send them to Vietnam, Annick and I had our first child, and fathers were not being drafted.

Now, all these years later, Annick and I have built up a whole repertoire of endearing names for each other—all in French, a language made for romance. They are loving. They are true. I always include one phrase that is both loving and true, though it may not sound very romantic.

Sixty Slices of Life... on Wry

I tell Annick that she is *mon sauveur de l'armée*, "my savior from the army."

New York / Virginia

23
A Better Way to Make Babies

When it turned out that the *International Herald Tribune* didn't want to hire me for their Paris office, or any other bureau, and that no one else in France or England wanted to hire me either, Annick and I moved back to the U.S., where job-finding was a comparative snap.

I first worked as assistant director of public relations for Prentice-Hall, the publishers, in Englewood Cliffs, N.J., then, after six months, became a reporter for the *Bergen Evening Record* in Hackensack. Six months later I was an assistant editor of *Senior Scholastic* and *World Week* magazines in New York City, and somewhere along the way the team of Annick and Fred Flaxman produced the first of two children we were to have.

Micky (Michel/Michael) was conceived in Paris and born in Teaneck, N.J. We did it the old-fashioned way, and as I recall all these years later, we rather enjoyed the process—at least the beginning of the procedure, if not the end.

Our first Franco-American baby looked so Chinese, he needed to undergo a total blood transfusion after only three days. Turns out his blood was incompatible with his mother's.

The doctor warned me that this was a very dangerous procedure at such a young age and that it could affect his brain. And I guess he was right, there, because Micky went on to get a doctorate from Harvard and he's now a professor

Sixty Slices of Life... on Wry

at M.I.T. That's undoubtedly because I donated the blood that replaced his original supply. If he had retained Annick's blood, he'd be teaching at a really good university now.

••••

When I was a kid my parents led me to believe that babies were born as the inevitable result of a man and a woman deeply loving each other. Would that it were so, all kids would come from loving parents and every toddler would be deeply wanted or he/she wouldn't materialize. That is, of course, how Annick and I created our two children. But, evidently, other people use different methods.

If there were such a thing as an All-Powerful, All-knowing God, surely He could have brought about a better way of making babies than a system of male plugs and female sockets. Not to mention menstruation and pregnancy. Why, any union electrician could think up a better plumbing process than that! And my metaphors are not nearly as mixed as God's methods of procreation. Do you have any idea, for example, how chickens do it? I used to have some and I still couldn't figure it out. Perhaps if I had had a rooster ….

It doesn't take a Divine Mind to conjure up a human reproductive procedure which would be superior to the one we're stuck with. Herewith four suggestions for improvements:

(1) If I were God, badly-wanted babies would appear as if by magic to loving parents in foam-lined, safety-tested, luxurious wooden cribs. No doctors. No hospitals. No pregnancies. No morning sickness. No medical bills.

I see no reason to get rid of sex, of course, but that act would never again result in procreation or disease—just fun. Instead of copulation, my requirement for having children would be a certificate in parenting. Doesn't that make more sense?

(2) My wife tells me that in France kids were taught that little boys were found in cabbage patches; little girls, under rose bushes. Perhaps there's some sexism inherent in the difference between those botanical locations. But this system seems preferable to me to finding each little boy and girl in a hot, dark, flooded sack under a totally different kind of bush, as is currently the case.

(3) Throughout the ages Northern European children were taught that babies were delivered by storks. Even that would be a better method than the one we have, as long as storks were made strong enough to keep our newborns from raining out of the sky.

Furthermore, if storks brought babies only to those couples who really wanted them and who would make good parents, this newly rediscovered ancient system of childbirth would be a clear improvement over what we now have in place.

(4) But, as long as we're talking about an Omnipotent, Omniscient, Omnipresent, Omnivorous God developing a birthing system, and He can do anything He wants, why doesn't He set up a toll-free 800 number so that couples can call Him directly to order the children of their dreams? Or give out a simple e-mail address (babies@heaven.god)?

Future parents could specify male or female, blonde or brunette, football player or musician, smoker or nonsmoker, window or aisle seater, etc. Couples could order babies with a built-in craving for crayfish or a passionate devotion to Paganini, infants who savor Schopenhauer or newborns with a preference for particle physics or Orthodox Judaism. Kids could come in as many different colors and styles as Chevrolets, with even more options.

Sixty Slices of Life... on Wry

As for those tingling sensations and warm feelings that men and women have now when they do what they do to make babies themselves, surely a God who is All-Good and Somewhat Imaginative could think of a way to make sparks fly between His creatures other than pumping male protrusions into female receptacles. But, if He needs my help, I'd be happy to come up with a few ideas.

24
Necktie Nightmares

I couldn't have imagined when I was young that I would have lived long enough to see the end of the Soviet Union. And now, it appears, I may even be around long enough to see the last days of something even older, more established and restrictive: neckties and jackets. I'm proud to say that I was personally responsible for this latest revolution.

The famous educator Horace Mann once said: "Be ashamed to die until you have won some victory for humanity." This is my victory.

Until a few years ago it seemed the average male executive would have preferred defeat to doing without his tie and jacket. In fact, he'd even wear this uniform to his grave. It's doubtful that an appointment with Lucifer, himself, in Boiler Room No. 1, would have gotten the true businessman or professional to loosen his knot and unbutton his collar.

So anyone suggesting that such a costume was inappropriate—not to mention uncomfortable—during the hot, humid days of summer was immediately suspected of being a communist revolutionary.

Yet nowhere was it written that white-collar men must wear ties and jackets. It was not one of the Ten Commandments. It was not in the Constitution. No law governing appropriate business dress was ever passed by Congress. I never encountered such an obligation as a stated company

Sixty Slices of Life... on Wry

rule or regulation.

We all knew that ties, jackets, and heat were a highly combustible mixture, and yet we continued to suffer summer after summer. The only thing that changed was the width of the ties and the lapels. Where was men's liberation when we needed it?

Of course ties and jackets do have their advantages. Jackets keep us warm in winter. They compensate for scrawny shoulders. They provide convenient pockets so that men don't have to carry handbags. And they help save tailors from extinction.

Ties cleverly conceal male tummies, which have a way of getting larger with each passing year. (Have you ever noticed that ties become wider at just the right point of the anatomy to conceal this fact?) Their manufacture keeps silk worms busy and the Italian economy flourishing. They give men's clothing designers something to design that puts their imaginations to use—which can't be said of jackets, pants and coats. And ties are the one garment in a man's wardrobe which gives him some room for fantasy and choice when he dresses in the morning.

But the businessman's uniform has always had its drawbacks. Jackets restrain natural body movements and must be removed to do virtually anything more energetic than eating. They are uncomfortable, even on cold winter days, when worn in overheated offices. Their sleeves cover up wristwatches, making it impossible to determine the time without alerting whomever you're with that you have something more pressing to do than be with them.

Wearing a tie is as pleasant as having a rope around your neck, and can lead to similar consequences. I've never known a tie which didn't like to dip itself in a bowl of soup, block the stream of a water fountain, or take in a sample of

Sixty Slices of Life... on Wry

spaghetti sauce, gravy, or salad dressing.

Do you have any idea how much time can be lost each morning, worldwide, by men tying and repeatedly re-tying their neckties—attempting, unsuccessfully, to get each end to come out the same length? Not to mention the accumulated hours wasted trying to select ties which go well with their shirts and jackets!

My own problems with ties and jackets go back to 7th grade when they were the required dress at the Horace Mann School for Boys in New York. They were supposed to make us behave like young gentlemen, I suppose, but didn't. There is only one type of jacket that will prevent boys from being boys—a strait-jacket. I ran for president of my class for four years on a platform that advocated abolishing the dress code, and won every time. But the ties and jackets remained.

When I was in my twenties, I commuted to downtown New York each day in a hot, humid, crowded subway. By the time I got to work, my shirt stuck to my body with the sweat created by my tie and jacket. Like everyone else, the first thing I did when I got to my office was to hang up my jacket and loosen my tie.

One day it occurred to me that, since I never actually wore my jacket at the office on hot summer days, the only purpose that garment served was to make me miserable in the subway. Did any of my fellow passengers really care whether I wore a jacket or not? So I started coming to work without one.

But then it seemed odd to be wearing a tie and no jacket in the subway. And the tie, tight around my neck with the collar button firmly closed, kept the heat in, continuing my discomfort. So I began traveling to work without the tie as well.

Sixty Slices of Life... on Wry

I was cooler in the subway and happier at work, but had to suffer some bad jokes and teasing from colleagues. After a week, though, there was someone else not wearing a tie. When another week passed, another office worker or two were tieless. Gradually the men with ties and jackets became the minority. A quiet revolution had taken place, and I had been its leader.

Even the women at the office appreciated what I had accomplished. After all, women rarely wore ties or jackets and men usually controlled the air conditioning system. The men insisted on keeping the temperature lower, to make up for their overdressing, making the women cold, uncomfortable, and justifiably irritable. When the men gave up their uniforms, they too were pleased to have a higher room temperature. This saved energy and money, and eliminated arguments over thermostat settings.

Later I moved to Chicago, which is more traditional and conservative than New York. Most of us commuted from our air-conditioned homes in our air-conditioned cars to our air-conditioned offices. My co-workers' ties and jackets stayed on. The women in the office were cold, uncomfortable, and justifiably irritable.

Weeks went by and I was the only executive who didn't wear a tie and jacket when the thermometer passed 75. No one followed my lead. No one joined my quiet, tieless, jacket-free call for revolution.

It made me feel a special kinship with the little boy in Hans Christian Andersen's *The Emperor's New Clothes*. He was the only one innocent enough to point out the obvious: the Emperor was not wearing any clothes. Businessmen, in the heat of summer, have been wearing too many.

But all that has been changing. The Horace Mann School for Boys is now also for girls, and ties and jackets

Sixty Slices of Life... on Wry

are no longer required. It seems that corporate down-sizing means more than laying off workers and managers. It means getting rid of ties and jackets, too—and not only for those who have lost their jobs. Informal dress at work is a benefit more and more companies are discovering and offering. It makes their remaining employees happier and more comfortable, it reduces their energy bills, and it doesn't cost them a cent.

I almost never wear ties and jackets anymore. I gave most of my ties away to my sister-in-law, who cut them up and used them in artistic quilts that fetched thousands of dollars in a New York gallery. My remaining ties hang in the back of my closet like a colorful still-life, an unwanted artwork gathering dust in a wardrobe purgatory, waiting to be discarded permanently or to come back in style.

But I no longer commute to work in a downtown office. I no longer put up with subways or traffic jams. I simply walk down one flight of stairs in my house to my office. I could go to work in my birthday suit and only my wife would notice the difference.

As the Rev. Martin Luther King, Jr., said in a somewhat different context: "I am free at last. Hallelujah, I am free at last!" And yet he wore ties and jackets, didn't he?

25
A Unique Memorial to Uncle Bill

When our two children were very young and we wanted to get out to a movie or a concert, we needed a baby-sitter. My wife's relatives lived across the Atlantic in France and my relatives were a few hundred miles north of our Reston, Virginia, home. So we started out by doing what everyone else did who didn't have family living close-by, and hired neighborhood teenagers for the job.

We came back from our first movie in ages to learn that the baby-sitter we hired had permitted our four-year-old son to throw rocks off the balcony of our 10th-story apartment at the pedestrians below. This situation presented us with a difficult choice: Should we get rid of our baby-sitter or our son? From a financial point of view, we probably made the wrong decision, but we never saw that baby-sitter again.

A few months later we returned from our first concert in months to see that the five-year-old brother of our teenage baby-sitter, who came along with her as part of the deal, was having a great time—hammering nails into our oak parquet floor!

A third teenage baby-sitter invited her boyfriend to stay with her at our house. They spent the entire evening together alone in our bedroom with the door locked—more interested, apparently, in creating their own children than having anything to do with ours.

Sixty Slices of Life... on Wry

So we soured on the very concept of teenage baby-sitters. But how, we wondered, could we find a mature, responsible, reliable baby-sitter in this budding new community where older people were hard to find?

Just at this point, as luck would have it, the Lutheran Church built Fellowship House—a home for elderly, poor people—on property adjacent to the townhouse cluster we moved to after we demonstrated what a public menace we were in a high-rise apartment building.

We decided to put up a notice on the Fellowship House bulletin board seeking a baby-sitter. We expected a warm, friendly grandmother to reply. But there was only one response and it was from a tall, thin, retired railroad electrician in his seventies named Bill Cissel.

Although at first we wondered whether a lifelong bachelor was the best choice to look after our children, this immediately likable, gentle, soft-spoken man seemed completely at ease with kids—and totally trustworthy. Then, too, he was the only choice. Besides, he wore a hearing aid, so chances were he wouldn't be bothered by whatever our unpredictable, uninhibited children might come out with next.

Our new baby-sitter wanted to be called "Uncle Bill," and so he was, and he lived up to his honorary title. Every time he came over to sit, he brought presents with him that undoubtedly cost him more than he could possibly make from what he earned for the evening. He also came with his own popcorn cooker, and the smell of fresh popcorn became as closely associated with Uncle Bill in our minds as the stench of mothballs which always permeated his clothing.

Uncle Bill was an avid newspaper reader, and he always brought clippings with him. He cut out articles about how things used to be, pictures from the past, and other items he thought would interest the kids.

When my wife and I went out for dinner, Uncle Bill would bring TV dinners with him for the children and himself. Our son, Micky, remembers what a thrill this was for him and his sister, Tana. Their mother never used frozen foods when she prepared a meal! What's more, the TV dinners were eaten right in front of the TV set while watching television—a combination that was not normally permitted in our household. My wife felt that to truly appreciate a meal, you had to concentrate on it. Talking was tolerated, but TV viewing and reading during dinner were strictly *interdit*.

Micky and Tana don't watch Lawrence Welk any more, but if they did, I'm sure it wouldn't be the same without a TV dinner on their laps. And, during the commercials, they'd want to hear stories about what it used to be like working on the railroad.

When Tana had a moment alone with Uncle Bill, he would tell her that she was his favorite—and not to tell Micky. When Micky had a moment alone with Uncle Bill, he would tell Micky that he was his favorite—and not to tell Tana. But I have the feeling that Uncle Bill was telling both children the truth.

Most of the people living in our neighborhood were young parents with professional jobs in Washington, D.C. Micky and Tana didn't know many older people, or people who worked with their hands for a living. This made Uncle Bill even more interesting, even more special.

After many months of coming to our house, Uncle Bill started inviting us to visit him in his apartment. None of us has ever forgotten the experience. Piles of newspapers were everywhere. Plastic covers were on everything. The

Sixty Slices of Life... on Wry

windows were closed, even during the hot, humid days of a Virginia summer, and there was no air conditioning. The stuffy atmosphere, combined with the ever-present, overpowering smell of mothballs, guaranteed that our visit would never last more than a few minutes.

Uncle Bill was our exclusive baby-sitter for as long as the children needed one, and a friend of the family long after that. When the kids were old enough to stay by themselves, we would invite Uncle Bill over anyway to have dinner and spend the evening with us. He continued to bring popcorn for dessert, and, after the meal, would fix anything that had broken since his last visit. He also brought his own knife sharpener to make sure our cutlery was always in shape.

At one of these dinners, Uncle Bill noticed that all the knives in our contemporary, Scandinavian flatware collection were dull. Before we knew what had happened, this kindhearted, helpful, saint of a man had his sharpener out and was working his way through the set, irreparably scratching the shiny surface of each and every blade.

Shortly afterwards we moved from Reston. Uncle Bill sent picture postcards to the children and commemorative stamps for Micky's collection. We received birthday and Christmas cards from him, and we sent him a copy of our family newsletter every December.

One year we received a handwritten reply to the newsletter from Uncle Bill's sister, whom we had never met. Bill Cissel had died.

We don't know where Uncle Bill was buried and, even if we did, it is likely to be very far from where we are living now. But we don't need to visit his grave site to be reminded of Uncle Bill. He has a much more unique memorial, one that comes with us wherever we go. His one mistake left permanent marks on our cutlery—and our

Sixty Slices of Life... on Wry

souls. And we are still full of warm feelings for Uncle Bill at every meal, with each and every use of our contemporary, Scandinavian, scraped and scratched knives.

26
Saying "No" to TV

When our son Micky was 10 and our daughter Tana, 6, they caught that terrible disease that has plagued youngsters (and some not-so-youngsters) ever since television sets first came into our homes—videoitis. This ailment's principal symptoms were clear: a complete inability to stop staring at an illuminated picture tube, no matter what was on it, combined with an intense craving for anything seen advertised, as long as it was unhealthy, unnecessary or unaffordable.

Doctors, hospitals, pills, and syrups were all out of the question. We tried gold star awards, allowance incentives, and outright bribes. But none of these methods worked.

One day, by chance, I discovered a very simple but effective means of treating this affliction. We happened to have an old-fashioned Zenith console with two doors covering the screen, each with a U-shaped handle. While cleaning out the garage, I came across a padlock I still had from my gym locker in high school. It occurred to me that the lock might just fit around the two handles. It did.

I wasn't trying to stop my children from watching television. My goal was simply to limit its use, to teach our kids to be selective and to spend at least some of their time doing active, creative things—like playing, for example. Or maybe even some homework. In my wildest fantasies I even imagined them taking out the garbage or drying the

Sixty Slices of Life... on Wry

dishes. But then I've always been a dreamer.

Some parents, faced with this problem, have gone so far as to get rid of their TV sets altogether. I think that is as foolish as letting kids watch television all they want. After all, there are worthwhile TV programs as well as worthless ones, and children can learn a great deal from television, just as they can from books. Besides, that wasn't an option that was available in my case, since I worked in public broadcasting and had to know what was on.

So Annick and I set up some simple ground rules: Our children could each watch only one hour of TV a day. But they could look at anything they wanted—well, almost anything.

Tana, our six-year-old, had little difficulty adjusting to the new house rule, but our 10-year-old boy at first deeply resented the limitation on his viewing freedom. I even recall being compared to a certain recent German leader—Adolf Hitler, I think it was.

But the kids had to do something with the time they were not spending watching television, and they did. Micky practiced the piano (without nagging), created fantastic buildings with wood blocks, mastered a labyrinth game, and joined a soccer team.

Tana painted one picture after another, played for hours with characters from outer space she made herself out of clothespins and corks, and even spent a great deal of time reading.

In short, they both found time to be children, to use their imaginations, and to get outdoors for fresh air and exercise.

After only a week they even forgot to check the TV listings, and sometimes days would go by with the padlock firmly in place. Micky's resentment subsided, as did most

Sixty Slices of Life... on Wry

of the pressure from both kids to buy products they saw advertised on the tube.

All this happened many years ago, when commercial television broadcasters had a different sense of social responsibility toward the next generation than they are exhibiting today. Those were the days when Captain Kangaroo and Mr. Wizard could be found on commercial stations and it was against FCC regulations to base children's programs on products they could buy.

Now—when entire programs seem to serve as half-hour toy commercials, and the educational content of network children's programs has been reduced to about zero—I wonder why more parents don't find a way to lock their TV sets or hide them from view.

As for us, we still have the padlock and we kept the old Zenith for many years. But our children are now old enough to control the TV set, the stereo, and the refrigerator, too. And Tana has two daughters of her own.

But she doesn't have a TV set.

27
Introducing the Classics

When our kids were growing up, I had a theory that, if I just surrounded them with classical music, they'd naturally grow to love it. This was one of several parental practices I stubbornly clung to, despite all evidence to the contrary.

I played Fauré for my children when they were fetuses, Enescu when they were infants, Bartok when they were babies, Tartini when they were toddlers, Bizet as they became bigger, Paganini for their puberty, and Albinoni as they reached adolescence. But that didn't stop them from preferring The Who when they were in the womb, the Beatles when they were babies, the Grateful Dead as they grew up, and God knows who now, since I can't tell rock from reggae.

I also surrounded my kids with public television and important books, with the same spectacular lack of success. When my daughter was a teenager, she watched soap operas on commercial TV and wouldn't have read *The Survival of the Human Race* if the survival of the human race had depended on it.

Though I didn't discover it until it was too late, I was doing everything wrong. If you want to raise a child to enjoy public TV, you've got to click past PBS as if those letters stood for Prurient Broadcasting and Sex.

If you want him to read *Moby Dick*, buy a copy and

Sixty Slices of Life... on Wry

make sure he sees you putting it back in the family safe after taking a quick peek at its mysterious pages.

And if you want your teenager to listen to classical music, firmly forbid the stuff from ever being played in your house. That's the way to get kids to catch on to Khachaturian.

As a society we've said "no" to drugs for a long time, and look where it's gotten us. Today it's hard to find a youngster who hasn't tried one. The logical thing, then, is to slap an "X" rating on every classical album. Do that and it won't be long before crack dealers will be selling *Coppelia*, potheads inhaling Puccini, and methamphetamine addicts turning on to *Mathis der Maler*.

We all know what the First Law of Adolescent Behavior is: *teenagers want whatever their parents dislike, and crave that which is prohibited.* So just say no to classical music and teenagers will listen to Bach instead of Bowie, Sibelius rather than Springsteen, Ravel will cost $100 dollars a copy via the French Connection, opera will go underground, concertos will replace cocaine, and symphonies will save our society.

Washington, D.C.

28
Barcarolle No. 1

My first job in public broadcasting was at WETA-TV in Washington, D.C. At the time the station was located on the campus of Howard University and WETA had no radio outlet. I commuted from Reston, Virginia, picking up my colleague, Mary Jane Phillips, on the way. We would talk and listen to the commercial classical music station, and the trip would pass quickly and enjoyably, despite the rush-hour traffic.

In the middle of our conversation one morning the radio station started to play the *Barcarolle No. 1* by Gabriel Fauré. Since we were talking when the announcer introduced the short piano piece, I didn't catch who the performer was.

"Mary Jane," I said, interrupting her at the end of a sentence. "Listen to this piece. It is a beautiful little gem that almost no one knows. I happen to have a recording of it."

We listened and, to my surprise and disappointment, it was performed so badly, I thought it was being ruined.

"Oh, Mary Jane," I said over the music. "I'm sorry, but this pianist hasn't the foggiest notion of how to play this piece!"

As soon as the words left my mouth I realized that I was certain to regret the comment. The pianist was sure to be Arthur Rubinstein or Vladimir Horowitz or someone as famous and highly respected as that. But I had no idea how

Sixty Slices of Life... on Wry

embarrassing the remark would turn out to be, until the piece finished and the announcer came back on the air.

"You have just heard Gabriel Fauré's *Barcarolle No. 1 in A Minor, Opus 26*," he said, "as performed by the composer."

I tried to recover quickly.

"Well, Mary Jane," I said, "it just goes to show you that the composer isn't necessarily the best interpreter of his own work!"

29
Birth of a Station

When I started my new job as special assistant to the general manager of public television station WETA in Washington, D.C., in 1968, my first assignment was to write a letter to the FCC asking for a six-month extension of our permit to construct public radio station WETA-FM 90.9. This was a more difficult task than you might think because we needed the extension due to a lack of money to activate the station. But the FCC would not accept that as an excuse, since in order to get the construction permit in the first place you were supposed to have the funds on hand.

So I wrote the letter. I don't remember exactly what I said, but it worked and we got our extension. Whatever the acceptable excuse I thought up was, I knew I could only use it once, so I asked Bill McCarter, WETA's vice president and general manager, if I could take on as my next assignment raising the funds to build the station. He gave me the go ahead. I was only 28 or 29 at the time and still inexperienced enough in fund-raising to imagine that I could pull this off.

In those days you could get 75% of the funds to start a public radio station from the U.S. Government's Department of Health, Education and Welfare (H.E.W.). The grants were competitive and the application was nearly the size of a telephone book. It included plans for construction,

Sixty Slices of Life... on Wry

engineering, programming, personnel, and financing the operation for several years in the future.

I put all this together, submitted it, and, much to my amazement, we received the grant. The other 25% of the funds required as the station match were probably produced by our creative accounting department.

Bill asked me to lead a search for someone with a knowledge of classical music and radio broadcasting whom we might hire as the first manager of the radio station. I scrounged up a few résumés without putting too much effort or time into the process and walked into Bill's office with the results.

"Who do you recommend for the job?" Bill asked as he glanced at the pile.

I laughed, paused, and gave him a one-word answer, "Me," after which I laughed some more, and Bill joined in.

But he took my recommendation, and that started my transition from writer to broadcaster.

To make a long story short, we managed to get the station on the air in April, 1970, and we even succeeded in stealing very good professional broadcasters away from higher-paying commercial stations. Since I couldn't propose much in the way of money, I offered creativity instead—the opportunity to produce their own programs, write their own scripts, do their own editing, provide their own engineering, answer their own phone calls, use their own records, make their own coffee, and clean up after themselves when they were through with their own, one-person shifts.

They did all this without complaint—except for cleaning up after themselves—and the station attracted a large audience of loyal listeners after just a few months on the air.

One of the first people I hired was Matt Edwards,

Sixty Slices of Life... on Wry

imported from New York City, the original, though short-lived, host for the "A.M." classical music program and the mind behind a weekly program called "Experiments in Music."

Matt was a proponent of anything new and avant-garde. But he understood that mixing this kind of music with the rest would probably turn off many, if not most, potential listeners. So we decided to segregate atonal, electronic, weird, strange and bizarre types of modern music into this one, discreet hour, broadcast once a week at noon, with a repeat the same night at 7. This way, listeners who wanted to try contemporary serious music would know just where to tune for it.

When we first went on the air we were monitored fairly frequently by the FCC to make sure we weren't violating any rules. As fate would have it, the first such auditioning took place in the middle of "Experiments in Music." There was a single selection scheduled on the program that day—a one-hour excerpt from a 19-hour electronic work which, like Ravel's "Bolero," repeats the same theme over and over again with an imperceptibly small change in each variation.

To the uninitiated ear of an FCC engineer, as well as other ordinary people, it sounded as though the record was stuck in its grooves, playing the same difficult-to-stomach passage over and over again. When the engineer tried the station that evening after 7 and heard the same repetitious sounds, he concluded that the record was still stuck. So he sent an inspector out to the station to see whether someone had died at the controls.

Matt went back to New York shortly after that and Bill Cerri, who was doing a jazz show for the station each evening, took over the early morning classical music shift, where he remained until his death in 1990.

30
Renee Chaney & the Police

Another of the original WETA-FM personalities was Renee Chaney, previously an audio engineer for the Library of Congress Music Division. There weren't many women on Washington radio in 1970, and most of them worked for WETA-FM.

Believing as I did in equality of the sexes, no special arrangements were made for Renee, even though her program, "Classical Grooves," was broadcast live, nightly from 11 p.m. to 1 a.m. As she had an FCC license to do her own engineering, she was often alone at the station at sign-off.

Add to this Renee's soft, sweet, seductive delivery and you had a potential problem. Male listeners were falling in love with her sight unseen. Seeing her would have made the problem nothing but worse, since she was one of those rare radio personalities who look as good as they sound. (I, of course, hired her because of her knowledge of classical music and audio engineering.)

For the four-and-a-half years that I ran WETA-FM, the station was housed in a small red brick structure at the base of its transmitting tower in an otherwise residential area of Arlington. A local company donated a trailer to house Bill Cerri's desk and the record library. My office was in a very small kitchen which was still used by the staff to make coffee and heat up meals. On the other side of the wall was the bathroom. When someone flushed the toilet,

Sixty Slices of Life... on Wry

I had to put callers on hold because I couldn't hear what they were saying. But no one else had any office at all.

Renee found herself all alone in the broadcast studio, connected to the world by the most powerful radio station in the Eastern United States—and by the telephone.

She could handle the 75,000 watts without thinking twice about it. It was the telephone which caused all the problems. There were calls from:

• *Heavy-breathers*, turned on, I assume, more by Renee's voice than by the chamber music recordings she played.

•*Highly-upset neighbors*, annoyed that they were receiving our FM signal on their AM radios, their TV sets, their toasters and their false teeth. (It was a powerful station—especially if you lived just across the street.)

• *Insomniacs,* somehow insensitive to the sleepy sounds of a serenade by Schubert, who phoned to ask a question, offer a suggestion, or blurt out anything else they could think of as an excuse to talk to Renee.

• *And one disgruntled former WETA-FM employee* whom I fired after he showed up for work stoned one night and then didn't show up at all the next. Renee was more afraid of his threats than all the heavy-breathers, neighbors and insomniacs put together.

So, after putting our ever-growing audience to sleep with Satie's *Gymnopédie No. 3*, Renee called the Arlington Police Department. They obligingly sent an officer over each night to make sure that Renee wasn't harmed as she left the building. Renee liked one of them so much, she dated him.

A rumor started circulating that Renee Chaney carried a gun. It wasn't true. Or necessary. She had a uniformed, armed escort to carry it for her.

31
Support for Public Radio

It is the lot of a public radio station to have to raise its own operating funds from its own listeners. This is done through a form of over-the-air begging called "membership week" or "pledge week," both of which last as long as a month. The staff asks the listeners to send in their support to the station and become "members."

"Members" get the same programs over the same frequency at the very same time as non-members, but they pay—sometimes handsomely—for the privilege. Remarkable as it may seem, thousands of people are willing to do this. Understandably, nine out of ten listeners do not. They are known in the trade affectionately as "freeloaders."

One day, after a solid week of making such requests during a "pledge" period, I received a small, gift-wrapped package in the mail from Cohen's Quality Shop in Alexandria, Virginia. I had never been to that store and didn't know anyone who worked there, so I opened it very carefully in case it was a plastic bomb from someone who was as sick and tired of our fund-raising appeals as I was.

The box contained a little note and a large jockstrap. The note said:

Dear Mr. Flaxman:

I am a steady listener of your station and I really enjoy the classical

Sixty Slices of Life... on Wry

music and Jean Shepherd's Show at night. One thing puzzles me, however. You keep asking your listeners to send in their support. Well, here's mine. I don't know how it will help the station, but you're certainly welcome to it.

Bob Marks

I wrote Mr. Marks a thank-you note right away, just as my mother taught me to do whenever I received a gift:

```
Dear Mr. Marks:

I literally do not know how to thank
you for sending us your support. I
realize that some listeners are so
loyal to our public radio service
that they would give us the shirts
off their backs.  But never, ever,
in the two years that WETA-FM has
been on the air, has a listener gone
quite this far!  May I simply assure
you that we shall use your support to
uphold all that is nearest and dear-
est to our non-commercial, non-profit
hearts.

Sincerely,
```

Fred Flaxman

```
Fred Flaxman,
Director of Radio
```

Sixty Slices of Life... on Wry

32
The Saturday Night Massacre

Richard Nixon—inadvertently, I'm sure—was responsible for what looked like my last day at WETA-FM.

On Saturday night, October 20, 1973, he fired the special Watergate prosecutor, Archibald Cox. Like many other Americans, I spent Sunday glued to the television set, wondering what was going to happen next. "The experts" were all being interviewed, but they were saying that whether or not impeachment proceedings began against Nixon would depend on the reaction of the public, and no one knew exactly what that would be.

I sat there thinking: *You're the head of a public radio station in the Nation's Capital. What should your station be doing at this historic moment? Playing Mozart's Requiem?*

And my inner voice replied: *Help answer the question everyone's asking today: "What does the public think?"*

So, starting when we went on the air at 6 a.m. the next morning, and continuing throughout the day, we broadcast a listener survey. We asked our audience to call us and let us know whether or not they thought impeachment proceedings should be begun against President Nixon. We promised to relay the results, whatever they were, to all area senators and representatives. We stated forthrightly that this was not a scientific poll, but rather an informal inquiry of the opinions of our own listeners who chose to call.

I did this entirely on my own initiative, without

Sixty Slices of Life... on Wry

consulting Don Taverner, the man who succeeded Bill McCarter as president of WETA. Don had been brought in, when Bill left to head WTTW/Chicago, to solve WETA's financial problems. He tried to do this by saying "no" to every request for money. And it became such a habit that he replied negatively to most other requests as well. I was sure he would have vetoed my listener survey idea. So I didn't ask him.

By the end of the day WETA-FM had received almost 4,000 calls. Some 98% of them favored initiating impeachment proceedings. We announced the results on the air late that evening, and I fully expected to be dismissed at any moment.

But when I walked into the WETA executive staff meeting the next morning, my fellow department heads shook my hand and congratulated me on WETA-FM's publicity coup. The radio station's poll had made the headlines in *The Washington Post*.

Don grumbled a bit and asked me some questions on the wording of the survey and the letter to the members of Congress. But he could hardly fire me while everyone else was singing my praises, so it turned out not to be my last day at WETA-FM, after all.

That happened more than a year later. When it came, it was due to a promotion, not a dismissal. I was asked to return to WETA-TV to become program director. It appears that when you try something daring in broadcasting, you can be fired if it fails—and rewarded if it works. Fortunately for me, WETA-FM worked well from the beginning.

33
Christmas in August

I've always felt that public radio and television should be innovative, and I encouraged my staff to come up with new ideas. So when Bill Cerri suggested that we play Christmas music in the middle of a heat wave in August—"to psychologically cool down our listeners"—I went for it. What's more important, so did our audience. "Christmas in August" became an annual WETA-FM tradition.

The event was scheduled in advance, so that it could be listed in the WETA program guide. It was so indicated for the morning of August 10, 1974. This, as fate would have it, turned out to be the day after President Nixon became the first and only President of the U.S. (so far) to resign from office.

Now I never had any particular love for Richard Nixon. But I have always felt strongly that public broadcasting stations should be politically neutral. So when my clock radio—set permanently to FM 90.9—woke me up to the strains of "Joy to the World" that morning, I was upset. I did something I had never done before, and haven't done since. I called up and criticized an announcer while he was still "on shift."

I thought that Bill should have changed the programming scheduled for that morning, or at least not played "Joy to the World" just after the news. He disagreed, and yet obeyed my instructions. But not without comment. He

Sixty Slices of Life... on Wry

announced over the air that "Christmas in August" had been abruptly cancelled ... by "Ebenezer Flaxman."

34
Steambath

I was not responsible for bringing Bruce Jay Friedman's *Steambath* to public television, but I was responsible for airing it on WETA-TV. The general manager at the time, the very same Don Taverner who didn't fire me for conducting the impeachment poll when I headed the radio station, had refused to broadcast it. He called the program "blasphemous" and "obscene."

Six months later, when I became program director of the TV station, I screened the play, and thought that it was one of the funniest, most creative, most imaginative programs I had ever seen. True, it had a few controversial language choices. True, God was presented as a Puerto Rican steambath attendant. And yes, Valerie Perrine was shown without any clothes. Nevertheless, as I felt the language was not that offensive, purgatory as a steambath was an interesting concept, and Ms. Perrine didn't look too bad with nothing on, I concluded that this program should be broadcast. But how could I do that after what Taverner had said about it? Especially that he had been quoted in the *Washington Post!*

Turns out that many months before this came up, WETA had formed a Community Advisory Board which had never met. Taverner had personally selected the members. I went to him and said something like this:

"Don, you think *Steambath* violates the moral standards of the community. But you are not from this community. You are from Maine and you have only lived here a short time. You appointed a Community Advisory Board and one of their functions is supposed to be to let us know what the standards of the community are. Why not set up a screening for them and ask their advice? It will make them feel useful and appreciated."

He reluctantly agreed to do this, but set up the session for 6 p.m. the next day or the day after, selecting what seemed to me to be a difficult time for people to attend the meeting, and giving them short notice.

When the appointed hour came and I saw, for the first time, the members of the Community Advisory Board as they filed in, I thought to myself: *I now understand why Don agreed to this. He selected these people to begin with. There isn't anyone under 100 years old in this group. There isn't a single black person. They all look like members of the National Organization for Decent Literature. The screening hasn't even started and I already know that I've lost!*

The meeting began with a five-minute speech by Taverner, letting everyone know how he felt about the program, prejudicing the case as much as possible. Then the lights went down and the show began.

It is one thing to watch a comedy on television in your living room by yourself, and quite another to see it with an audience in a movie theater. That is why TV comedies make use of "laugh tracks." When other people are there to laugh and do so, it makes you want to laugh, too. In this case, I could tell as we sat there and screened *Steambath* that the audience was enjoying the play. I could hear them laughing out loud at all the funny parts. No laugh track was needed!

When the program ended, the lights were turned back on, and Don asked for comments. One committee member

Sixty Slices of Life... on Wry

after another got up to speak. They all raved about the program and said how much they personally enjoyed it. All except one little old lady in the back row who said that she didn't like some of the language and she was disturbed by the nudity. But even *she* felt the play should be broadcast for those who wanted to see it and who weren't bothered by the content.

And that is how and why *Steambath* was broadcast over WETA-TV, and how I missed the opportunity of receiving Don Taverner's ax once again. Not long after that, Don himself obtained the ax he had so often promised to give to us.

35
My Dinner with Bibi

When I was a teenager in the 1950s, I loved to go to New York City to see Swedish movies—not because they were deeper and more intellectual than the Hollywood variety, though they certainly were, but because they were more likely to have nude scenes.

The 1950s were not at all like today. Girly magazines were not common—at least not where I grew up, right across the Hudson River from New York. American films and television in those days were quite prudish. Pornography was banned entirely and, although X-rated movies were rumored to exist at private bachelor parties, you certainly couldn't find them in a public movie theater.

So I was very curious as to what, exactly, a female, human body looked like—without clothes. This curiosity was heightened by the fact that, aside from my mother, all the members of my immediate family—my father and two older brothers—were males. Even the dog was masculine. And my mother was completely inhibited about her body—which was not what I really wanted to look at in any case.

To make matters worse, I was sent to an all-boys private school during the fall, winter and spring, and to all-boy athletic camps in the summer.

God was I curious!

The movies of Ingmar Bergman did a great deal to

Sixty Slices of Life... on Wry

satisfy that curiosity. The young women in these "art" films were blond, blue-eyed and beautiful, even if the pictures themselves were about the plague, death, and the meaning of existence. Bergman used the same actresses over and over again, and I almost felt I got to know one of these recurring stars personally. Her unforgettably sexy Swedish name was Bibi Andersson.

Bibi. Oh, Bibi. How I dreamed I could see a girl like Bibi in the flesh one day—for real!

A quarter of a century passed. I had long since married and made real progress in overcoming my curiosity on the subject of female anatomy. But I never lost my fascination for foreign films. One of the first things I tried to do when I became a public television executive was to create a PBS series called *International Playhouse* to present outstanding telefilms from around the world.

I was looking for a host for this series when my brother, John—who was a TV, film and theatrical producer in New York—suggested that I consider Bibi Andersson for the role.

"Bibi Andersson!" I replied. "But she must be 105 by now!" I thought that because she was a mature Swedish woman when I was an immature American boy, she must be ages older than I was.

"I saw her at a party the other day," John said. "And she looked great. If you're interested in talking to her about hosting your series, I can arrange for the two of you to meet."

At the time Bibi Andersson had an apartment in New York and I worked in Washington, D.C. So, on the appointed day, I took a Metroliner for the Big Apple. I ate some peanuts from the snack bar on the train and worried that they would make me break out the way they did when

Sixty Slices of Life... on Wry

I was a teenager.

When I arrived in New York it was pouring, and I didn't have an umbrella. By the time I walked from the subway to Bibi's apartment building to pick her up for our dinner meeting, I was soaked.

The doorman announced me from the lobby, and Bibi Andersson was waiting for me in the hall when the elevator doors opened at her floor. I thought she would look like she had just walked out of "Smiles of a Summer Night," but she seemed, although good looking, rather plain, average even, and, except for her accent, American.

"Would you like to come in, dry off, and have a drink first?" she asked, as I dripped all over the plush carpeting.

It was the maid's day off, as it happened, and so there we were—Bibi Andersson and I—all alone in her apartment.

"I have an idea," she said. "Instead of going out to a restaurant in this rain, why don't we eat here? I had a huge party yesterday and there's all this food left over. Seems a pity to waste it. Would you mind helping me finish it?"

Would I mind? Really!

Bibi started waiting on me, serving drinks and dinner while we talked about everything under the sun. I did most of the talking, and she was the world's best listener.

At one point, when I was going on and on about the problems of public television, she interrupted me. "Excuse me, please, half a second," she said, "while I get a pencil and paper. I want to write down what you just said."

From then on she took notes from time to time, and I was as profound as I could manage to be.

Was I a great conversationalist, or was Bibi just a terrific actress trying to get a part she wanted from a visiting producer?

Sixty Slices of Life... on Wry

This is a question that occurred to me only later. At the time I was pinching myself to be sure I wasn't dreaming—or getting a pimple on my chin from those greasy peanuts I had eaten on the train.

Then Bibi started telling me about the autobiography she was working on. "It's strange," she said. "I'm writing about my teenage years and just thinking about that period is beginning to give me acne again!" As she spoke, I saw that she had a small zit on the side of her chin which I would not have noticed otherwise.

I don't remember what we had for dinner, but I do recall that Bibi spilled the coffee as she served dessert. Apparently the established, world-famous Swedish actress was even more nervous about this meeting than the inexperienced, unknown Washington producer.

After dinner, I offered to help Bibi do the dishes, since the maid was off. And there we were, in Bibi Andersson's kitchen, side by side, washing and drying pots and pans. *Had I died and gone to... a Swedish movie set?*

Bibi Andersson would have been the host of *International Playhouse*, except for a bit of a problem I was never able to overcome: funding the series. And I never saw Bibi Andersson again—except in Swedish films, of course, where she belongs.

In Ingmar Bergman's production of *Confessions of a Fool*, a four-part Swedish telefilm I wanted to use in *International Playhouse*, Bibi appeared completely in the buff.

I undoubtedly would have had to cut out that scene. But I would have done so most reluctantly. What about the teenage boys out there who are curious about female anatomy and who have two older brothers and a dog who's also a male? What does public TV do for them?

Sixty Slices of Life... on Wry

Perhaps curiosity disappeared with the sexual revolution of the last fifty years. Perhaps today it is amply satisfied in the bedrooms rather than the movie houses of America.

And perhaps Bibi Andersson is somebody's grandmother by now. But, over the past few years, I have been collecting her films on video. In this medium, Bibi will remain young and beautiful forever. And I can go back to being a teenager once again.

France Again / Bulgaria

36
From Paris with Love

There are, of course, many advantages to being married to a French woman. I won't elaborate on these. Some things are best left to the imagination, and Americans have always had quite an imagination when it comes to French women. But I shall mention one distinct benefit here: the excuse—no, the necessity—of making trips to France as often as possible. While our children were growing up and I had the kind of steady income I can only vaguely remember now, we tried to visit Annick's family every two years.

On one of these trips, while watching a particularly funny 15-minute comedy on French television, it occurred to me that the PBS audience in the U.S. would enjoy this material, too, if only they had a chance to see it. Then it dawned on me that there were probably not that many American public TV executives who understood French well enough to select excerpts from French TV programs to show the PBS audience. For all I knew, I might be the only one. And that's when the idea for *From Paris with Love: An Evening of French Television* was born.

I was vice president for national programming at WETA-TV in Washington, D.C., at the time. My job was to develop programming from WETA for national distribution over PBS. Always strapped for funds, WETA would find *From Paris with Love* an ideal project. It would be inexpensive, since it would involve putting together excerpts

Sixty Slices of Life... on Wry

from existing programs rather than starting from scratch. It would be attention-getting, since PBS had never presented an evening of foreign television before. It would be practical to work on, since the French embassy was in Washington. And, for me, it would be a source of several all-expenses-paid trips back to Paris!

I arranged for the first of these voyages with the cultural attaché. The French government paid my way via Air France and put me up at one of the best hotels in the "City of Lights," a stone's throw from the Arc de Triomphe. The purpose of the trip: to explore the possibility of working with the three government-owned TV networks there were in 1978, to see if they would supply the excerpts I would select; to convince a government-sponsored cultural agency called Inter-Audiovisuel to supply the funds required; and to interview an American-born independent producer living in Paris to see if he would work with me to carry out the project.

The producer came highly recommended to me by WNET, New York City's public TV Channel 13. They had just worked with him on a documentary project. Tim Thomson (I'll call him here to protect the guilty) was a handsome black man with a beautiful bass voice, who had grown up in Seattle. But he had been in Paris for many years and spoke French more perfectly than any American I had ever heard who didn't have French-speaking parents. He was a trained singer with an obviously good ear for language. In fact he sang French the way the French do when they speak, and used all the slang expressions you're never taught in class.

When I met Tim he had been an independent producer in Paris for three years. Before that he had been a foreign

Sixty Slices of Life… on Wry

correspondent for one of our major TV networks.

Tim was living the high life. He and his wife had an apartment in the seventh arrondisement, one of the best residential sections of Paris. He drove me around town in a Ferrari convertible. He treated me to a five-star restaurant where I dined on pigeon, to me the least offensive of their gourmet offerings. I'll bet even the pigeon was surprised to learn he was worth so much money.

Tim also took me for lunch at the Club du 44 Avenue Foche, where he was the only American and the only black member. He was also, undoubtedly, the poorest member. Others, as I recall, included an Arab who had just purchased the S.S. France for use as his private yacht.

Before lunch, Tim took me on a tour of the club, which had its own luxuriously modern building a short walk from the Arc de Triomphe. There was an indoor swimming pool surrounded by tropical gardens. There were special rooms for exercise and massage. But what I remember most, all these years later, is the bar. Not that I can tell you what that large room looked like; just that it was filled with the most stunningly beautiful women I had ever seen all at one time in one room, and each and every one of them was drinking … alone.

"Who are they?" I asked Tim quietly and discreetly on our way through the room.

"Oh," Tim replied casually, "they are kept by the club. They live upstairs. They are there for the members."

For an independent producer, Tim Thomson certainly seemed to be doing OK. I remember thinking at the time that he was either so successful money didn't matter to him any more, or that he was so in debt, it didn't matter either.

Tim was hired as the line producer to take care of things in Paris while I ran the show as the executive pro-

Sixty Slices of Life... on Wry

ducer from Washington.

I then interviewed Evelyne Leclercq, the beautiful and charming blonde "speakerine" from TF-1, the largest French TV network, to see if her English was good enough to serve as our host. She would be filmed on location around Paris, bridging the excerpts Tim and I were to select. On French television at the time, "speakerines" came on your screen between programs, sitting in an easy chair in the studio surrounded by flowers, and told you about what was coming up later in the schedule. (I once asked why there were no male "speakers" providing this service, but that evidently was such a bad idea, it had occurred to absolutely no one.)

I hired Evelyne, though, as it turned out, they couldn't understand a word she said in Texas. It didn't matter there, of course. All that counted was how she said it and how she looked as she said it. I went back to Washington with the feeling that my project was in good hands in Paris.

Once in the States I arranged with PBS to have three hours of prime time the following July 14th—Bastille Day. No one really knew whether there would be much of an audience for dubbed and subtitled excerpts from French TV programs but, hey, it was better than yet another summer repeat and, anyway, July 14 was always one of the worst nights of the year to try to attract a TV audience.

I made a second French-government-sponsored trip to Paris to sit with Tim in screening rooms all over the city watching videotapes of French TV programs: comedy, drama, music, cultural documentaries, ballets, operas—anything and everything that might interest a PBS audience. We made our selections, attempted to get the rights to broadcast the material, and then tried to get good copies of the excerpts for transfer to our U.S. video system.

Sixty Slices of Life... on Wry

For example, we managed to get the rights to a colorful ballet called *Les Mariés de la Tour Eiffel*, only to find that the program had been made on film and there was a scratch from one end to the other on the only remaining copy. We learned to identify substitutes for every program we selected.

I returned to Washington to write the script. Shortly afterwards, 42,000 francs (about $9,000 at the time) were turned over to Tim who, as the producer, was to pay Evelyne, himself, and other nontechnical expenses for the program.

That was the last we were to see of Tim Thomson. He and the francs disappeared quickly and completely.

He was to show up very visibly a few months later—anchoring the morning news on a network affiliate in Los Angeles.

Inter-Audiovisual came up with money a second time to pay Evelyne Leclercq. And, horror of horrors, I had to return to Paris yet another time to serve as the producer for the videotaping of the opening, closing and bridges.

••••

My idea for the show's open and close was to make a music video with Jacques Brel singing his song *les Prénoms de Paris*. We would illustrate Brel's poetic words with video, and crawl the credits over these images. As Brel sang in French, our visualization would help our American audience to understand the song.

The words have a lot to do with love in Paris: a couple walking hand in hand, the first kiss in the Tuileries gardens, that sort of thing. We had one day to shoot this material—in the morning from a van driving around the city; in the afternoon from a small boat we rented to take on the Seine.

It was a beautiful, warm sunny day in May. Paris in

Sixty Slices of Life... on Wry

the spring. Ideal for our shoot.

We drove first to the Tuileries and no sooner did we get the camera out of the van and set it up on its tripod than a young couple walked hand-in-hand down the path in front of us. They have been walking hand-in-hand at the beginning and end and intermissions of my program ever since, even though, for all I know, they may have split up later that same day.

But they never stopped and kissed; not, at least, while they were in range of our camera. So we spent the rest of the morning driving around Paris, looking for embracing lovers—without success.

During our lunch break we discussed the problem. We were going to be on a boat the rest of the day. If we didn't happen to catch any lovers kissing along the banks of the Seine, we would have used up our time and resources and still be missing an important shot for our program. We decided we had better cover ourselves by staging the scene.

But we had no actors with us. There were just the three of us: the cameraman, the sound engineer, and me. I was the only one without equipment to operate, so it was agreed that I would play the part of the male lover. For the female lead the cameraman graciously volunteered his girlfriend, whom he called from the café phone. I don't think she really liked the idea, but she came anyway and did what she was asked to do, begrudgingly.

And that is how it came to be that I made an Alfred Hitchcock-like appearance in my own television production, passionately kissing a young Parisian woman I had just met moments before, and doing this to the music of my favorite French singer/songwriter.

It was a challenge to explain this incident to Annick. Deciding that a good offense was the best defense, I called

Sixty Slices of Life… on Wry

her from Paris to tell her the story immediately, weeks before she would see the results on the screen. She believed me, but it wasn't until she finally saw the program that she had any idea of how good an actor I can really be—given the right role.

Somehow my talents were never discovered by Hollywood, and the only parts I have played since were cameo roles in other programs I produced. If I don't give myself on-camera roles, who will?

••••

Evelyne Leclercq came to the U.S. for the first time to attend a preview of *From Paris with Love* at the French Embassy and to make a tour of several cities to promote the special.

She arrived at Kennedy International Airport in New York, where all she had to do was to change planes for the trip to Washington. She never even went downtown. But she did have to take a taxi with her suitcases from one terminal to another.

The fare came to just over two dollars. Evelyne thought that she handed the driver three one-dollar bills, so she told him to keep the change. He looked at the money, thanked his passenger without further comment, and promptly took off.

Unlike American paper currency, the French bills Evelyne was used to were a different size and color depending on their denomination.

Evelyne soon realized that she had handed the cabby three $100 bills.

••••

Some 500 newspaper and magazine articles were written about *From Paris with Love: An Evening of French Television*. The program was carried by 229 PBS stations

Sixty Slices of Life... on Wry

coast to coast from 8 to 11 P.M. EDT on July 14, 1978, or later that week. It was the second highest-rated program fed by PBS that week.

It was viewed in almost as many households as the most-watched program that week, a *National Geographic Special*, and by more people than *Masterpiece Theatre*.

The average viewing time in the 4,010,000 households which tuned in for the program was 74 minutes. With more than one viewer per household, *From Paris with Love* may have been watched by some 6- to 8-million people.

That's a lot of folks witnessing me kissing a woman who was not my wife.

37
The French Connection

Before leaving for Paris on one of my business trips for *From Paris with Love*, I asked Annick what she would like me to bring back from France. More than anything else, she wanted a box of real French flour. French flour, you see, is different from American flour. If you want to make French pastries, bread, and croissants which taste as good as what you find in Paris, you must have French flour to succeed.

Well I was so busy looking at French TV programs and talking to executives for those two weeks, I forgot all about buying a box of flour until the Saturday night before my Sunday departure back to the States. In fact it wasn't until I was packing my suitcase that I remembered Annick's request.

I was staying with French friends in their apartment. The stores were closed for the day and I wasn't going to have time to go shopping before rushing out to the airport first thing in the morning. So I accepted my friends' kind offer to take their nearly-full box of flour with me.

Since this box had been opened and I didn't relish the idea of white flour getting all over my clothes and everything else, I sealed the box carefully with tape, put it in a tightly wrapped plastic bag which I also secured with tape, finally putting all this into a paper bag which I sealed securely as well.

Sixty Slices of Life... on Wry

During the flight, when it came time to hand out the customs declarations forms, an extra sheet was distributed which apologized in advance for how long it would take to get through the formalities. The notice explained that there was a terrible drug abuse problem in the U.S. and the custom's service had been instructed to do all it could to keep illicit substances from entering the country.

The inspection lines were indeed long and slow-moving after landing in Washington. When, at long last, it was my turn to go through, I started getting nervous about my box of flour. I wondered whether French flour was permitted in the U.S. I worried that the white powder might look like heroin and that, as a 37-year-old, single man with a swarthy complexion, travelling alone, coming from Paris, I would be a prime candidate as a potential drug trafficker.

The custom's officer asked me to open up all my bags, then started riffling through my suitcase. Hidden under my clothes in the far right corner he came across the carefully sealed bag with the flour box inside. As he started tearing off the paper, I thought I had better explain what he was about to discover there.

"M ... m ... my wife is, is French," I said. "Sh ... she is a very good cook, and, and I l ... love real Fr ... French pastries ..."

The custom's inspector had the paper bag off and was removing the plastic without looking up at me.

"Sh ... she a ... asked me to bring her b ... back s ... some Fr ... French fl ... flour...."

He was opening the box itself now, apparently not listening at all to me, and he was just about to take a look at its contents.

"I was staying w... with fr... friends...."

Sixty Slices of Life... on Wry

The inspector poured a bit of the white powder in his hand. The expression on his face at that moment was one I'll never forget. He looked as though he, single-handedly, had just uncovered a billion dollar supply of heroin and prevented it from reaching the streets of America. He was undoubtedly thinking about the award and promotion he was going to receive when he signaled for an agricultural department inspector to come over.

That inspector, fortunately for me, knew the difference between heroin and flour, and I was neither delayed further, fined, nor imprisoned.

The French pastries Annick made with that box of flour were delicious. But they were still not as good as the ones you find in France. Turns out French water is also different, as is French butter, French sugar, and French salt.

All this explains why we have never had a problem of excessive immigration to the U.S. from France.

38
French Fried in Belgium

Since *From Paris with Love: An Evening of French Television* turned out to be a bigger success than anyone had ever anticipated—myself included—I decided to see if I could carry out the same idea with the country next door: Belgium. I figured I could at least speak one of the two languages they used there, and all the Flemish speakers seemed to be fluent in English. But the problem of the two separate cultures inhabiting a single nation turned out to be *my* biggest challenge as well as *theirs*. At one point, it almost prevented *An Evening of Belgian Television* from happening at all.

The Belgian program was done with both the RTBF, the French-language television network, and the BRT, the Flemish service. Though they were both located in separate, but equal, identical wings of the same television center on the outskirts of Brussels, they had never before worked together on a project. I realized from the start that both cultures would have to be treated separately but equally on my program as well, so it was designed to be a two-hour special—the first consisting of excerpts from RTBF's programs, the second featuring a drama from the BRT.

The problem which nearly killed the project came up as a result of my desire to use the famous Belgian singer/song-writer Jacques Brel behind the closing credits. The second hour was supposed to be either in Flemish with

Sixty Slices of Life… on Wry

subtitles or dubbed into English. No French permitted. Although Brel, who was from Brussels, could speak both languages, he was associated more with French culture, especially since he moved to Paris and wrote and sang almost entirely in French.

Yet he had recorded a song he wrote called "My Flat Land" in Flemish, which is what I proposed to use under the final credits. "My Flat Land" is roughly the equivalent of our "America the Beautiful," a romantic ballad, full of love for one's country, which has become the unofficial national anthem.

The day came to pass that the entire two-hour program was almost finished when the Belgian Ministry of French Culture learned of my plans to end the special—and had a hissy fit. They threatened to withdraw their share of the funds underwriting the project unless Brel were to sing "My Flat Land" in French!

I pointed out to them that I was only trying to be fair to both cultures and that we were talking about the second, Flemish, hour of the program. I didn't point out to them that no one in the U.S. would care whether the music under the credits at the end was in Flemish or French: they wouldn't understand either. And I didn't point out to them in French, Flemish, or English what I thought of them for threatening to withhold their share of the costs.

The French Culture ministry said that it didn't even know that Brel had recorded "My Flat Land" in Flemish, and insisted that the French version was the one which was always played and should be used. They seemed to think it was a sacrilege to have him sing this patriotic song in some other language. It was as though someone had proposed doing *An Evening of American Television* for broadcast on Belgian TV and ending the show with "America the

Sixty Slices of Life… on Wry

Beautiful"—sung in Yiddish!

The fact that *An Evening of Belgian Television* was completed and broadcast over PBS on April 26, 1980, was thanks to the sound thinking of the sound engineer assigned to the project—and to the good luck that Brel's recordings of "My Flat Land" in both languages were sung in the same key at the same tempo, using the same orchestration. The engineer edited together a recording of "My Flat Land" that Brel never made where the verses alternated between French and English. It worked so well, you could swear Brel made the recording that way to begin with.

• • • •

Working late at Belgian Television on the Brel language problem caused me to miss dinner. I returned to the nearby bed-and-breakfast where I was living for the month at 10 p.m. with severe hunger pains. As there were no places to eat out at that time in the neighborhood, I asked the kind, friendly, elderly, French-speaking lady who ran the B&B and served the breakfasts in the morning if she could do me a big favor and cook a couple of eggs for me to eat. I knew it was not included in the price of the room, but I was perfectly willing to pay extra—to do anything, really—to stop my stomach pains.

She was happy to do this for me, she replied in her usual, cheerful manner, and asked me how I wanted the eggs prepared.

After eating her delicious rendition of poached eggs on toast, I asked her how much I owed her.

"Owe me?" she replied as if I had both surprised and insulted her. "Nothing, of course. What do you think I am, a *Jew*?"

Now *I* was the one who was surprised—and shocked speechless. I realized that this sweet old lady, who had just

Sixty Slices of Life... on Wry

been so kind to me, meant me no harm. She was just using an old, if blatantly anti-Semitic, expression in the French language. This was before the days of political correctness and sensitivity to minorities even in the U.S., much less Belgium and France.

It was difficult for me to speak at all, but I managed what now became a great effort to thank her. Then I went up to my room with a full stomach and an empty heart.

39
Bulgarian Diplomacy

I'm allergic to springtime. When the leaves reappear on the trees after a long winter, the grasses turn green, and the flowers emerge from nowhere, I start sneezing, my eyes begin to itch, and my chest clogs up. Without the help of various pills, sprays, and drops, I would start to wheeze, sleep would become impossible, and accomplishing anything beyond merely staying alive would be out of the question.

I'm particularly bad in the month of June, so when Annick and I took off for Bulgaria at precisely that time of year in 1979, I made sure I brought half my medicine chest along. This country, after all, is known for its roses, and the kind of seasonal allergy I have is called "rose fever" for a reason.

I was sent to Bulgaria as the official guest of Bulgarian State Television on a little-used State Department cultural exchange program. Only one American had been on this program before me—a long-haired, bearded guitarist, five years earlier—and he had not been heard from since. This did not seem to matter, however, because Bulgaria was not considered a very important country, and there was a surplus of long-haired, bearded guitarists in the U.S. at the time.

Knowing nothing about Bulgaria, and having never been behind the Iron Curtain before, I read everything I

Sixty Slices of Life... on Wry

could get a hold of on the subject. Bulgaria, I discovered, was the most Stalinist of all the Eastern European countries—a nation that was particularly adept at getting rid of its exiled dissidents with the use of poison darts at the ends of umbrellas which "accidentally" hit people as they tried to cross bridges in London. Sounded like an interesting place to visit.

The night after we arrived, the president of Bulgarian Television gave an official dinner in my honor. It took place around a large round table filled with higher-ups from the Ministry of Culture and Education and Bulgarian Broadcasting, plus their interpreters. Some of the Bulgarians spoke English, some French, and others nothing but Bulgarian. Whenever anyone uttered the slightest little nothing, it took ten minutes to get it translated all around the table.

And there were a lot of little nothings to be said because there were a lot of toasts with a lot of Bulgarian plum brandy, and each time a toast was made everyone was expected to go bottoms up.

This was particularly difficult for me because I am not a drinker. I never touch alcohol unless I'm put in a social situation like this where it seems almost insulting to refuse to participate. Although I couldn't get myself to do "bottoms up," and sipped as little as possible of this firewater with each toast, I nevertheless felt it rapidly going to my head. I started to wonder if I had any idea what I was saying to my esteemed hosts.

The president of Bulgarian Television kept making toasts, and I was expected to respond with my own. So I made my debut as a diplomat, praising such noncontroversial ideas as peace, brotherhood, friendship, and cooperation.

Sixty Slices of Life... on Wry

However, each time I uttered one of my banalities, the president shook his head grimly from left to right as though he totally disagreed with everything I said.

I started to worry that I was actually saying the opposite of what I thought I was saying. All of a sudden, I had a splitting headache.

I usually don't get headaches at all, never mind migraines. But this was the worst one, by far, that I had ever experienced. And yet the toasts kept coming, and I kept replying. I smiled at the official on my left. I smiled at the interpreter on my right. I smiled at the president's wife across the table from me. And I felt I was making my debut as an actor.

My throbbing head became unbearable, yet the toasts went on. Peace. Brotherhood. Friendship. Cooperation. AGONY!

What could I do? How could I get out of this without letting down my country, my flag, public broadcasting, and my own honor by admitting that I was ... sick?

To this day I don't remember a single item on the menu of that meal. Only the plum brandy. But I stuck it out to the end.

In the taxi afterwards on the way back to the hotel, I asked Annick if she had noticed my predicament. She was completely surprised to learn I had a problem. Two things then occurred to me that I had totally forgotten about.

The first was that my allergy pills contained a warning on the label not to drink alcohol after taking this medication. That explained the splitting headache.

The second was something that I had read about Bulgaria in the dossier the State Department had supplied me with before going there: that it was one of only three countries in the world where shaking your head from left

Sixty Slices of Life... on Wry

to right meant "yes" and nodding your head up and down meant "no."

The president of Bulgarian Television was in favor of peace, brotherhood, friendship, and cooperation after all.

40
Gastronomically Challenged

When I was a little kid, my two favorite meals were spaghetti with meat balls and hot dogs with French fries. I have made some culinary progress since then. I am now 69 years old and my first and second choices for dinner are [let's hear the fanfare!]: (1) spaghetti with turkey meat sauce and (2) sausages with mashed potatoes.

As a youngster I ate very little and was always the skinniest boy in my class. I liked almost nothing. I didn't even care for ice cream and chocolate. I dislike today much of what I detested then, except that the more I hear about cholesterol, heart attacks, and cancer, the more I seem to crave sweets, red meat, and sauces.

I'm no longer a kid, and I'm no longer skinny. My French wife, who is a superb cook by all accounts, has been trying for years to expand my culinary tastes without doing the same to my waistline. She has made very little progress on either front.

Perhaps I exaggerate a little. I do like a few Chinese dishes which I wouldn't touch when I got married, and there is one item on a Thai menu I can enjoy. It's made with a peanut sauce, which is as close to peanut butter as the Thais are going to get. The rest consists of sliced chicken bits barbecued on what looks like Texas-sized toothpicks. Now that's my kind of food.

But, by and large, the way some people are physically

Sixty Slices of Life... on Wry

or emotionally retarded, I appear to be gastronomically fixated at the level of a five-year-old. Over the years, this has caused me a good deal of embarrassment.

Once I was invited to a box lunch with Japanese and American television executives at Japan House in New York. Beautiful, lacquered, wooden boxes were provided by the Japan Society, and they were truly works of art. One was waiting patiently on the table in front of each of us, each exquisite box covered by a matching lid.

As the lunch began, we opened our boxes. Much to my horror they contained picture-perfect displays of raw sea food—sushi. I was at a complete loss: I never eat cooked seafood, much less raw fish! I really thought that if I put so much as one bite in my mouth, I would ruin everyone else's pleasure with what I would involuntarily do next.

All the others around the large conference table oohed and aahed with pleasure. How could I escape?

I talked to the Japanese TV executive on my left, and I talked to the American TV executive on my right. In between, I stuck chopsticks into the opened box in front of me, moving the sticks quickly from the box to my mouth, chewing the air at the end of the sticks, and monopolizing the conversation as much as possible in order to spend as little time as I could pretending to eat.

To my great relief, I noticed that as the guests finished their sushi, they put their lids back on their boxes. I did the same, thus avoiding humiliation, if not starvation.

I don't know why I'm so afraid of foods I'm not used to, but I went to a party once which gave me a clear indication that my problem is psychological rather than physical. The hors d'oeuvres I sampled looked like meatballs, but tasted even better. They were so delicious I made the mistake of asking the hostess what they were made from.

Sixty Slices of Life... on Wry

"Chopped crab meat," she replied.

I couldn't eat another one.

Then there was the time I was invited for dinner at the swank Paris apartment of one of France's most famous TV personalities, Evelyne Leclercq. Americans rarely give dinner parties any more and when they do, they rarely serve seafood. But that's not only what Evelyne selected for the appetizer. She also served fish for the main course. To make matters worse, she had prepared it herself!

I apologized profusely, fibbing that I was allergic to fish and seafood. Evelyne quickly made a hamburger for me, and I don't know who felt worse about the situation. Ever since, my wife and I have learned to mention my "allergy" to anyone still foolish enough to invite us to dinner.

Being culinarily underdeveloped is not recognized as a disability, except, I suspect, by those of us who suffer from this affliction. We have no support groups, no doctors who know how to treat us, no reserved parking spaces in front of gourmet restaurants.

No one sympathizes with us when we are invited to Chez Panisse in Berkeley, Calif., and would rather be eating at Hiram's Hot Dogs in Fort Lee, N.J. No one feels sorry for us when we are treated to the best dining establishments in Taipei while we would rather be slurping down noodles in that city's exciting night market. No one cares that we suffer a million humiliations every time a friend invites us for dinner, unless that friend is four years old; or that we're forced to suffer in silence, victims of retarded taste buds which would rather sample a strawberry milkshake than a bottle of the finest French champagne; or that everyone is sure we are recovering alcoholics because we won't touch a glass of wine.

Why isn't there a National Association for the Ad-

Sixty Slices of Life... on Wry

vancement of the Gastronomically Challenged? Why aren't government grants going to scientists to study how to get people like me to eat gherkins with gusto or pompano without pain?

Although, as of this writing, there has never been a Jewish, Hispanic, or female U.S. President, there have been at least two culinarily-retarded White House residents in recent memory. George H. W. Bush championed our cause when he said, "I didn't like broccoli when I was a child, and I don't like it now, and I'm President of the United States and I don't have to eat broccoli if I don't want to!" Maybe he would agree to head our support group? And we could make the late Richard Nixon our honorary founder. He liked to eat everything with ketchup, just like my eleven-year-old granddaughter. And, before his bypass operation, Bill Clinton was well-known for his love of fast food.

If the gastronomically-deprived followed my lead and came out of the closet, we might find that, at least in America, we're not a minority after all. As McDonald's, Pizza Hut, and Kentucky Fried Chicken spread throughout the world, it won't be too long before a huge new generation of food Philistines takes over the known universe. And I'll finally be able to hold up my head with McPride.

41
Mischief in Paris

Because I owned a beagle from the age of 8 until he died 14 years later, I had always thought of myself as a dog person. As it's turned out, however, I have had only one dog in my life and—what is even more unusual—just one wife. But I've had several cats—none of which I asked for or wanted.

The first, Mischief, was a gift of my French sister-in-law, Sylvie, when my family and I spent a year in Paris. Our daughter, Tana, who was 10 at the time, was very upset by being forcibly separated from her friends and moving from Reston, Virginia, the only environment she had ever known. Sylvie thought having a cat might help.

Mischief was a grey, striped tabby. He turned out to be well named, and not just because he seemed to have the letter "M" on his forehead. He was a trouble maker from Day *Un*.

We had rented a furnished apartment in a modern building not far from the Arc de Triomphe on the right bank of the Seine. But the apartment was decorated in a very ornate, Louis-the-14th style. Tassels dangled from the upholstery of all the chairs and sofas, and one of Mischief's favorite activities was making these move back and forth. They frequently got caught in his paws and thus inadvertently removed from the furniture.

The woman who rented us the apartment was not

Sixty Slices of Life... on Wry

likely to notice an occasional missing tassel, but the situation quickly passed the occasional stage to the point where there were very few tassels left.

Worried that Mischief's paws would continue to cause irreversible damage—and that we would have to pay the replacement costs which would result— Annick got on the phone with a lady veterinarian to see about having the cat's claws removed.

"I don't do claw removals," the vet said coldly. "If you want a pet with no claws, get a snake." And she hung up.

Annick, humiliated, gave up the de-clawing idea immediately, and we were forced to move to an apartment with less valuable furnishings.

••••

As the new apartment wasn't very far from the old one, and we didn't have the wherewithal to hire a mover, I rented a van and did everything myself. This was the first (and so far, you'll be happy to hear, the last) time I have ever driven a truck. I wasn't at all used to its width, nor was I accustomed to the narrowness of the streets of Paris.

My ten-year-old daughter was sitting next to me as I made my way along one of these streets which had cars parked over the curb on both sides, leaving just the narrowest of passages for vehicles driving one-way up the center.

As we drove along, I heard a strange cracking noise on the right side of the van. *Crack, crack, crack, crack.* I asked my daughter if she could see what was making the racket.

She looked out the window, then turned back and said to me, perfectly calmly: "Oh, Daddy, that's just the noise the side-view mirrors on the cars make as they snap off when you pass them."

Sixty Slices of Life... on Wry

It served those drivers right for parking illegally.

• • • •

After a year in Paris, my family—democratic as it is—took a vote on whether or not to return to the U.S. I wanted to stay, but was outvoted 3-1. The children were very homesick and my French-born wife, after having lived in the U.S. for 15 years, was the true "Ugly American," complaining about how everything in France worked or, more often, didn't.

When we returned to the States, Mischief, of course, came with us. We lived for one more year in Reston, then moved with him to Tucson, Arizona, driving all across the country in our car. Each day we found a place to stop for an hour so both cat and family could run around and get some exercise. Problem was, when we were ready to move on, Mischief wasn't. One day we lost three hours looking for him after he decided to play hide-and-seek, with him doing all the hiding.

We started thinking about giving up and moving on without him, but were afraid what that might have done to our sensitive young daughter's mental health—and our future relationship. So we made sure that Mischief was back safely in the car before we continued on. And there were no further exercise stops before arriving at our new home.

We managed to get our feline friend from Paris all across the Atlantic Ocean to Reston; then we succeeded in moving him across the continent to Tucson, which was even harder. But, unfortunately, this particular cat's story ended near our new home in the desert, not very long after our arrival. Mischief got out of the house one evening and got himself into real, terminal mischief.

We never saw him again, and, in the middle of that night, we were awakened by the sound of coyotes howling.

Arizona / Illinois

42
Meow Tse-Tung

My family and I lived in the Southwest for only three-and-a-half years, but we enjoyed every minute of it. We took advantage of several short vacations to explore our new state thoroughly. We visited the south rim of the Grand Canyon on one trip; the north rim on another. We went to Canyon de Chelly, Lake Powell, and the Organ Pipes National Monument.

One summer we managed to leave Arizona and get back to France for four weeks. When we returned, we had no sooner walked in the front door than we heard a strange sound coming, it seemed, from the middle of the chimney. I opened the flu door, and out dropped the dirtiest, most emaciated Siamese cat I have ever seen. He must have climbed up the roof, fallen down the chimney, and been trapped there for several days … or several weeks.

We fed, watered, and cleaned this cat and Tana, who was only 11 at the time, named him Meow Tse-Tung.

But after eating and drinking everything in sight for four days, Meow disappeared one day as suddenly as he had appeared, and we never saw him again.

We assume he went back home, wherever that was, and to his position as Chairman of the Communist Party of the Felines' Republic of China.

43
Cat Calls

When my family moved to the Chicago suburbs so that I could take a job as vice president for national program development for WTTW, our daughter found an emaciated kitten that she promptly named Ribsey. (All these years and moves later, Ribsey has become a truly fat cat and his name has taken on a distinctly ironic tone.)

Local telephone service in our Glenview home was provided by Illinois Bell. Knowing that we didn't have enough to read, this magnanimous company was kind enough to send us a little publication called *Telebriefs* with our phone bill each month.

It was by dutifully reading this freebie one day that I finally came to realize that I am not at all like a lot of pet owners. An article titled *When your pet's alone, pick up the phone and call* began with these enlightening words:

"If you're like a lot of other pet owners, you probably wonder how your pet is getting along when you're at work."

I became somewhat fond of our latest unrequested cat, but I never once thought about him when I was at work.

The piece then continued to assure me that I could and should communicate with my cat anytime I was away from the house. "All you need is an answering machine," the article went on. "The rest is easy.

"Just dial your home number and let it ring until your

Sixty Slices of Life... on Wry

answering machine picks up the call. Listen for the beep, then start talking. You can address your pet by name, just as you would if you were home. It really doesn't matter what you say after that, because it's the sound of your voice that your pet appreciates the most."

I suspected that it was the cost of my call that Illinois Bell appreciated the most. They could have cared less if I babbled in Catabolic Pig Latin, so long as I paid by the minute.

But I admired their thoughtful concern for hearing-impaired animals: "Before you leave in the morning," they concluded this particular tidbit, "remember to turn up the volume a little on your answering machine, so your pet will hear you."

All this made me wonder why Illinois Bell didn't offer a telephone with a paw-size button which could be programmed to reach subscribers' office phones or any other number where they could be reached. That way, cat owners could find out how much their felines missed *them* during the day. And, if it were a whole lot, Illinois Bell's profits would soar.

America might have its homeless people and folks who go to bed hungry every night. We might have generations of jobless blacks living in poverty, without education or training, in deteriorating inner cities. But we're a caring society. We're concerned about communicating with our disadvantaged, speechless, lonely ... pets.

44
In Pursuit of "Pure" Gasoline

My wife and I went on a vacation in Connecticut. We decided to make the two-day drive from the Chicago area, rather than fly, because we thought we had a better chance of leaving and arriving on time, and felt it would be safer and more comfortable. We also figured we had a slightly better chance of not losing our luggage. But we didn't count on the knotty ethical problems we would encounter buying gasoline along the way.

When we first noticed we were getting low on gas we were in the middle of rural Indiana. We exited from the toll way, paid our share of the road repairs, and drove to the only gas station in sight—Exxon.

"We can't buy Exxon," I said to my wife. "Not after what they've done to the coast of Alaska." She agreed, so we drove on a back road for what turned out to be seven miles to the nearest village. They had a general store with a gas pump. Thank God it wasn't another Exxon, because our gas gauge was already in the red warning zone. It was Amoco.

"We can't buy Amoco," my wife said. "Not after what they've done to the coast of Brittany." Annick was born on that French coast, which was devastated by an oil spill from the Amoco Cadiz. I wanted to remain happily married, so we headed back to the toll way and continued on to the next exit.

Sixty Slices of Life... on Wry

That ramp led to a Mobil station. "Wonderful," I said. "They underwrite *Masterpiece Theatre* on PBS. Let's fill 'er up."

"But I don't want to pay for all those far-right political messages Mobil buys in newspapers and magazines all over the country," Annick protested. "Besides, we haven't seen *Masterpiece Theatre* in years." [Since then Mobil, now ExxonMobil, dropped its underwriting altogether, and we've started watching *Masterpiece* again.]

Before we drove on, I used Mobil's men's room. I mention this only so I can tell you about the graffiti I saw on the electric hand-dryer there. The machine was carefully labeled with simple instructions for its operation:

"1. Shake off excess water from hands.
"2. Press button.
"3. Rub hands together rapidly under air stream.
"4. Machine turns off automatically."

Then a hand-written addition, neatly printed just below in indelible ink, said:

"5. Wipe hands on trousers."

But I digress.

We left the Mobil station and drove 23 more miles to the next town, holding our breath all the way. There we found a Sunoco station. "I don't want to use Sunoco," I protested. "I don't think they've ever underwritten a public television series. Let's see if we can find a Chevron dealer. They paid for those terrific Bill Moyers documentaries."

So we did another 13 miles of country roads. We were tired of the interstate highway, anyway. Then, between two

Sixty Slices of Life... on Wry

huge fields some agribusiness operator was being paid millions not to grow anything on, we ran out of gas completely and our car coasted to a halt.

"Well, we had better walk in the direction we were driving," I suggested. "We know how far the nearest gas station is the way we came."

So we continued on foot, frustrated that we had not been able to find a single gallon of ethically pure gasoline before running out entirely, but proud of ourselves for being socially responsible citizens.

About three miles later I saw what looked like a major intersection in the distance, and—sure enough—as we got closer we could see that three out of four of its corners were occupied by gas stations.

On the southwest corner was Exxon. Amoco was on the southeast. On the northwest corner was Mobil. And on the northeast corner was a bar.

We went to the bar. And I don't even drink.

45
No Soliciting

At home one night, right in the middle of a late dinner, the door bell rang and I went to see who was there. We weren't expecting any visitors.

I turned on the porch light, opened the door a crack, and looked right into the frightening, twisted face of a stranger waiting to get in. He was an enormous, powerful-looking man, the kind who looked like he would break you in two by accident if he so much as scratched his left ear lobe.

"Are you interested in lowering your electric bills?" he asked, without introducing himself.

"Yes," I said, because I'm not good at lying. And I invited him in immediately. What else could I do without looking as though I were prejudiced against burglars?

The moment he entered my home, I knew I had made a big mistake.

"I represent the CDL, the Citizen's Defense League," he said with an alcohol-scented breath as he quickly flashed what looked like an ID card. "We're fighting for lower electric rates, banning the use of pesticides in nursery schools and old age homes, and bringing prayer back to the home, where it belongs. We're the people who stood up to the banks when they tried to charge customers for going to the rest room without opening an account. We'd like you to sign our petition advocating no-fault divorce, no-fault

Sixty Slices of Life... on Wry

auto accident insurance, no-fault assault and battery, no-fault homicide, and no-fault police brutality."

"No-fault police brutality?"

"Well, yes. No one is really responsible for his behavior. Everything, you know, is the result of either heredity or environment. In either case, it's not the fault of the individual."

"But, see here," I protested. "I'm not going to sign a petition that sanctions assault and battery!"

"This doesn't sanction anything, fellow," he replied. "It just makes it quicker and easier to get these cases through the courts since no one has to determine where the fault lies."

"I see your point, but, I think there are more important considerations than court efficiency."

"Would you sign this anyway? All it asks is that the matter be brought before the public as a referendum in the next election."

"Really, I'd rather not," I said. "I'd like to save my signature for things that I believe in a bit more strongly, like sexual promiscuity and vitamin C."

"Well, will you at least make a contribution to the CDL?" he pleaded impatiently. "I haven't got all day."

"Why should I contribute to the CDL? I already contribute to the Citizens Utility Board, and they're fighting to keep the electric rates down, too."

"But they're not effective. You see how high your electric rates are. Are they getting any lower? We're committed to direct action, if necessary, to bring down power lines if that's what it takes to bring down electric rates. Anyway, we think utility poles are ugly."

"I don't disagree with you aesthetically, but ..."

"How about $50?"

Sixty Slices of Life... on Wry

"Fifty dollars? I've got a daughter in college. I can't afford ..."

"Thirty-five?"

"No, I told you I already contributed to ...."

"Twenty-five dollars, and that's my final offer." He looked like he was about to scratch his left ear lobe, but I held firm.

He got up, glanced at me in disgust, and walked straight out the door without even saying, "Good-bye." I breathed a sigh of relief, and started thinking how foolish I had been to let a total stranger in my house. What if he had asked to join us for dinner?

We shouldn't permit soliciting in our community, I thought to myself. It interrupts our peaceful, suburban lives and could be dangerous to our wealth. But what can we do about it? Then I got an idea.

The next day I went out and bought several "NO SOLICITING" signs in various shapes and sizes. Some, made out of plastic, were very inexpensive. Others were more costly because they were molded of metal or crafted in wood.

The next night I went door to door in our neighborhood selling these signs.

Most of my neighbors opened the door only a crack, suspicious, I suppose, that I had come to deprive them, one way or another, of their money or their lives.

"We don't allow soliciting here," they said in a universally hostile tone reserved for door-to-door salesmen who interrupt people after they've just sat down for dinner.

"Great," I came back without a pause. "I have just what you're looking for!"

46
A Real Test of American Citizenship

Once the law was changed and a French person could become a U.S. citizen without giving up her French nationality, Annick decided to become a dual-national. She filled out the necessary forms, studied the U.S. Constitution, took the test, and became an American citizen.

It's not that she would have minded at all giving up her French passport and the right to vote in France. It's that I didn't want her to do this. Being married to a French citizen, after all, gave our children dual-nationality and made it possible for any or all of us to live and work in France anytime we wanted to.

Also, with my Jewish heritage of suffering from persecution, I wanted to be able to escape the country should the U.S. ever be taken over by a government which discriminated against people who were not Christian, sanctioned torture, instituted imprisonment without trial for years at a time, tapped the phones of innocent citizens, and committed all kinds of other violations of civil liberties which, of course, could never happen here.

Any Tom, Dick, or Harry can be a U.S. citizen. All they have to do is make sure they were born within our borders or that at least one of their parents was an American if they entered the human race anywhere else.

It's a bit more difficult for any José, Hiroshi, or Vladimir. To become a naturalized citizen, you must wait five

Sixty Slices of Life... on Wry

years, fill out a long application form, and even pass a test to prove you have some knowledge of our government. Native citizens don't need to know anything—and often don't.

The application form Annick had to fill out was created during the McCarthy Era, and it reflected the values of that period. Every would-be American had to list every organization he had ever joined. But he also needed to know that the First Amendment to the Constitution guarantees freedom of assembly.

The form even asked if you had ever been a member of the Communist Party, a Nazi, a prostitute, or a criminal. Native citizens, of course, could be all of the above, without losing their nationality, although they might spend a little time behind bars.

The red scare and the yellow peril are now years behind us, and no one has found an American Communist under anyone's bed for more than half a century. To see a Nazi, you have to stay up very late and watch old black-and-white World War II movies on cable TV. The sexual revolution has reduced the demand for prostitutes, and AIDS has reduced their attraction, while crime has become so commonplace most of it doesn't even make the papers any more.

So it seems to me that instead of asking aspiring citizens what the three branches of government are, the application form should pose questions that determine whether they have really become 100 percent American or not. For example:

1) Do you say "have a nice day" after every goodbye—even to perfect strangers who, for all you know, deserve just the opposite?

2) Do you eat peanut butter and jelly sandwiches,

Sixty Slices of Life... on Wry

drink Coca-Cola, and stop at McDonald's at least once a week?

3) Do you call everyone by his or her first names, whether or not you have ever met before?

4) Do you get rid of every ache and pain by taking a pill, a syrup, or a drink?

5) Do you read fewer than two books a year, but spend at least seven hours a day watching TV?

6) Would you rather go to a baseball or football game than to a concert?

7) Do you agree with our major corporations that post-nasal drip, loose dentures, piles, and ring-around-the-collar are our most serious national problems?

8) Is your idea of a garden to have a few bushes next to your house with lawn all around, and your idea of success to have enough money to pay someone else to mow it?

9) Will you join the PTA, the Little League, the Girl Scouts, and the Rotary Club, and will you contribute each year to the United Way?

10) Will you swear or affirm that, if granted U.S. citizenship, you will buy two cars, a high definition digital TV, a home computer, an iPod, a laptop, and a Blackberry whether you need them or not? And promise to use credit cards for all your purchases?

Anyone answering "yes" to at least 7 out of these 10 questions is clearly an American, no matter where he was born or how long he has lived here, and should be entitled to all the privileges of citizenship.

But by this criteria Annick would never have been given her American passport. So I guess I should be grateful for the citizenship test just as it is.

According to my extensive research on the subject, the only instances of applicants not passing the existing test for

Sixty Slices of Life... on Wry

US citizenship are:

    1. The person who answered "Hindenburg" when asked who the first President was;

    2. The applicant who replied "Are you kidding?" when asked the name of the current American President; and

    3. The man who, when asked why he couldn't become President of the U.S., replied: "Because I am a Jew."

47
The Teen Disease

When our daughter was a teenager she went through a very difficult period during which she performed poorly at school and even worse at home. My wife and I tried everything from changing schools to switching psychiatrists, but nothing seemed to make any difference. Finally, after exhausting all other possibilities, we gave up. And that worked.

Our daughter improved dramatically starting the day we decided to treat her like the family cat—to appreciate her for what she was, love her, feed her, shelter her, hope she comes back at night, pray that she doesn't have any little ones ... and not expect anything in return.

At one time or another, it seems, most teenagers go through a period when they'd rather do anything than clean up their rooms, help around the house, do their homework—or any other kind of work, for that matter.

Before the development of psychology, their attitude would have been described as selfish, lazy, and rude. Now it's more fashionable to look at their behavior as evidence of low self-esteem, inferiority complexes, or, perhaps, hormonal change syndrome. But whatever you call it, dealing with teenagers ranges from difficult to impossible.

Since so many parents report the same symptoms, it occurred to me that these teenagers must be suffering from the same malady. I call it decentahumanaphobia (fear of being a decent human being), but you can call it by its common name, the Teen Disease. Consider it like the measles,

Sixty Slices of Life... on Wry

mumps, and chicken pox—something that most youngsters have to go through if they don't get inoculated against it. It's just part of growing up.

The trouble with the Teen Disease is that it is mental rather than physical, and there is no known vaccination against it.

The scientist who discovers a cure for this illness will receive the everlasting gratitude of millions of parents for generations to come, and will fully deserve the Nobel Peace Prize for all the domestic squabbles which will be avoided.

Can you imagine a pill that would make your son want to do the dishes? Or an injection which would compel your teenager to hang up her cell phone after no more than three minutes? Or a capsule that would make resentful youngsters appreciate the lifetime benefits of education? Or a syrup which would keep your daughter studying biology all weekend rather than practicing it?

I have great confidence in modern medicine's ability to come up with a cure for the Teen Disease, now that I've identified it. In the meantime, I offer the following practical suggestion for treating the symptoms:

Since teenagers, as is well known, get along better with anyone else's parents than their own, let's set up a teenage swap system. Parents could register their problem sons and daughters with this service. For a fee of, let's say, $500, Trade-a-Teen would arrange for their troubled teenagers to live with some other parents while another teenager came to live with them.

Compared to psychiatrists' bills, $500 is an inexpensive way of alleviating the worst effects of a disease which could prove fatal—to the parents, if not the teenagers.

It may be the only way.

California / Oregon

48
Sixty Days as a Columnist

Television is a very collaborative medium. It requires team work. It is creativity by committee. While I enjoyed my work as vice president for national program development at WTTW/Chicago, I missed the personal creativity represented by writing. So I started writing newspaper columns in my spare time.

Knowing that I was not an expert in any field, I thought my best chance of getting published was to write about every day modern life with a tongue-in-cheek approach.

My first attempt had to do with teenage girl behavior, a subject with which I was all too familiar at that time. I showed the results to friends, who thought the piece was very good. But friends are friends because they are supportive. So I decided to send the column to some editor who didn't know me. I thought I would start with the top, with a national publication, then, following rejection, to submit it to the *Chicago Tribune*. Assuming rejection there, I would try the local weekly *News/Voice* papers.

Much to my surprise, *The Wall Street Journal* accepted my column for their op-ed page. And the same was true for my second and third attempts. This was followed by publication of many more of my pieces by major city newspapers all over the country, and some magazines as well.

Next I got a weekly spot in the *News/Voice* chain of

Sixty Slices of Life... on Wry

suburban Chicago newspapers, which resulted in my receiving a first place award in the 1988 competition of the National Society of Newspaper Columnists.

That went to my head and I decided that I would rather be a full-time newspaper columnist than a public broadcasting executive. I subscribed to *Editor & Publisher* and for a year searched its classified ads in vain for a newspaper searching for a general interest columnist.

I sent my impressive collection of clips to the editor of *Newsday* on Long Island, New York. He responded that he loved my work and would hire me in an instant except for two problems: (1) he had no openings and (2) if he had an opening and he hired me, he would be strung up in front of his office by all the reporters there who had been waiting for years to become columnists.

Then finally it came: a classified ad from the *Sacramento Union* in California. And, to make a long story short, they hired me and I accepted the position at one-third the salary I had been making in Chicago.

The *Sacramento Union* was the oldest daily newspaper in the West. Mark Twain had once worked there.

On March 5, 1990, my first day of work, I went upstairs to the fourth floor to pick up my ID card. As I entered the lobby of the executive offices, a young man exited rapidly, stopped abruptly, and exploded with the loudest, most productive sneeze I have ever witnessed. I jumped, my heart skipped a beat, and my face must have given away unintended feelings of disgust, because he apologized immediately and introduced himself. He was Danny Benvenuti, the new owner of the paper.

"I'm your new columnist," I said, shaking his germ-infested hand as I introduced myself.

"Are you a conservative or a liberal?" he asked right

Sixty Slices of Life... on Wry

away, posing the black and white alternatives into which, I later learned, he divided the world and all its inhabitants.

I think pigeon holes should be reserved for pigeons, but that's not what I replied. "I guess you could call me a radical pragmatist," I said. "I believe in what works, and think we should get rid of what doesn't."

"Radical pragmatist," he repeated, as if he were giving serious thought to the concept. "A practical person. I like that." He gave me some advice about being completely sure of everything I wrote before it goes to press, concluding the one and only private meeting I have ever had with Mr. Benvenuti. I was fired two months later.

Three times a week I appeared on the front page of the local section, writing about everything from cholesterol to reincarnation (if you don't watch your cholesterol, you'd better believe in reincarnation). I advocated making April Fool's Day a national holiday (to commemorate all the foolishness we have to put up with the other 364). I wrote in defense of dishwashing (which, like sex, is most enjoyable when not performed routinely three times a day, and is both dirty and clean, depending on how you look at it).

I came out for flossing, against pornography, critical of the post office, and in favor of funding the Sacramento Symphony. I even suggested a simple way for parents to get their teenagers to start listening to classical music (forbid it). I wasn't exactly a leftist revolutionary. I might have almost been mistaken for a country club Republican.

But I did make two mistakes which, in retrospect, I believe led to my dismissal. First, I wrote a column against capital punishment when the paper's editorial position was staunchly pro-death penalty. Second, I submitted a pro-choice column on abortion which was never even printed. I was rewarded shortly afterwards with a phone call from

Sixty Slices of Life... on Wry

the editor informing me that my services were no longer needed.

The editor, Jim Vesely, a first-class professional with a lifetime full of newspaper experience, was asked to stay on when Benvenuti and his real estate partner purchased the paper. Vesely hired me to serve as the "ying" to the "yang" supplied on alternate days by a conservative Catholic who had previously been city editor.

"Columnists are like windshield wipers," Vesely explained to Benvenuti, who had no previous involvement with journalism. "A paper should have them going left and right, right and left, so subscribers can look straight through and get a glimpse of the truth."

But Danny Benvenuti had a different philosophy. He purchased the newspaper—and everyone on it. Why should he, a born-again Christian, spend his money paying someone to write columns with which he occasionally disagreed? Why should Benvenuti—who was young, good-looking, rich, and who had God on his side—listen to anyone else?

I had thought my role as a columnist was to give my perspective on events in as interesting, concise, clear and persuasive a manner as possible. Benvenuti, it seems, thought my job was to express *his* views. He won.

At least in the short term. But, two years later—tired, I suppose, of losing money by appealing only to ultra-right readers—Benvenuti and his partner sold the paper to a local printer. From a peak circulation of 115,000 in the 1970's, the *Sacramento Union* declined to only 31,500 when it folded on January 14, 1994.

While it lasted, I loved being a full-time columnist for a big-city, daily newspaper. I welcomed the chance to open readers' minds and challenge their thinking. And I

Sixty Slices of Life... on Wry

believe it was better to have had the ideal job for only 60 days than not to have had it at all.

But I do have one regret. I wanted to write a column satirizing the narrow-mindedness and antidemocratic tendencies of the religious right. I never got to it. Then again, I guess it doesn't matter. The *Sacramento Union* wouldn't have printed it anyway.

49
Chicken!

We built a home on 12 acres between Ashland and Medford, Oregon, with plenty of room for … chickens.

One drizzly spring day I drove past a farming supply store and couldn't help but notice a large, temporary sign hanging from their building: "FREE CHICKS!"

Well, I'm as much of a sucker for a bargain as anyone, so I pulled into their parking lot.

Six free chicks per customer was the deal; no strings attached. So I got a box and hand-picked three yellow ones and three dark ones. There were hundreds to choose from, all as small and as cute as they could be.

There were several other adults taking advantage of the give-away, but they were all accompanied by young children. No matter. I have wanted to have chickens ever since, as a child, I tasted truly fresh eggs at my uncle's house in the country. Now, by George, I was going to have them. Even if this wasn't exactly planned for. Even if I had no idea where I was going to put them when I got home.

So I purchased a heating lamp, a feeder, a waterer, and a 25-pound bag of starter feed. For $17, I had my free chicks, and I drove right home with them chirping happily in the back of my station wagon.

I forgot to ask what breeds they were, but I overheard the lady at the counter tell the man who was in front of me in line that they were all "broilers." So I'd have fresh meat, not fresh eggs, but, hey, they were free, after all, weren't they?

Once home I cleaned out an abandoned aquarium which served as an ideal home for my new chicks. A bigger problem was finding a spot for the birds where they wouldn't serve as a TV dinner for our two cats.

The solution turned out to be my home office. I just had to remember to keep the door closed at all times. When I received a business call from New York or Chicago, the chicks could be heard chirping in the background. That confirmed many a caller's impression that I had moved to the sticks and dropped out of civilized society. One client thought he had reached the wrong number: "Was this Teleflax Productions … or Flaxman Farms?"

Fortunately, I rarely had business meetings in my office, because, after a few days, the place definitely smelled more like Flaxman Farms than it did Teleflax Productions.

The chicks turned into chickens amazingly fast. My wife and I went on a ten-day trip to the East Coast. When we returned, the chicks had outgrown the aquarium and I had to change my priorities, put business commitments and thank-you notes on hold, and turn my attention immediately to building a chicken coop outside. I spent $18 for lumber and chicken wire, plus another $22 for poultry supplies, and my free chicks were chirping cheerfully again.

But not for long. Turns out that the life of a "broiler" is not measured in years or even months. I was advised by the helpful folks at the Grange that chickens should be, uhm, processed, after eight to ten weeks for best taste and tenderness. Now, there was no way that I was going to do the processing myself, nor could I delegate this task to my

Sixty Slices of Life... on Wry

wife without endangering many years of happy marriage, so I put in a phone call to Klaus Schulzke, my friendly, neighborhood butcher.

"How much do you charge to butcher chickens?" I asked, after some introductory remarks about the cold, rainy May we were having.

"Oh, I don't do poultry," he responded.

"You don't?" I sputtered, shocked by this surprising news. But then I regained my composure and asked: "Could you tell me who does?"

"I'm not really sure." He went on to explain that he knew of a couple of people in the area who used to do this, but he didn't think they did it any more. I got their names anyway.

My wife started joking that our meat birds would die of old age, while I got on the phone to the two names Schulzke had given me. He was right. Neither of these chicken choppers was in the business any more, but one did give me the name and phone number of someone who was.

It was with great relief that I made an appointment for our six chickens with Mary Jeter, whose business card identifies her as "The Chicken Plucker," and who proudly boasts that she is state certified. I had never talked to a state certified chicken plucker before, and I must say the conversation was most enlightening.

Turns out that Mary charged $1.55 or $1.65 per chicken, depending on the breed. In addition there was a $1 fee for the use and cleaning of their crate. In return the chickens are killed, de-feathered, cleaned out, frozen and packaged, ready for pickup a couple of days later. So it was going to cost me $10.60 to free myself from my free chicks, which, by then, should be two- to three-pound chickens.

Sixty Slices of Life… on Wry

Lest you think that I am some sort of heartless bird murderer, I hasten to add that before making this appointment, I talked to the chickens about the situation. I proposed a simple contract: *I feed you now and, in return, you feed me later. I take good care of you for your entire, if abbreviated, life, and you supply me with a few pieces of fried chicken and some leftover chicken salad afterwards.* Is it a deal?

That seemed fine with them. They continued chirping happily as if I had been talking about the weather. It occurred to me that one reason they were so happy is that they had something that most humans lack: a definite purpose to their lives.

Mary told me that on their final day, the chickens were not to be fed, just watered. So their last supper was on June 29, when I went out of my way to gather several handfuls of their favorite food—freshly-picked clover.

On June 30th my wife helped me catch the chickens and put them in our cat carriers for transport to the Chicken Plucker. It was their second and last trip in the station wagon. They were silent the entire way.

Our chickens were smaller than the other birds we saw when we arrived at the pluckatorium. They were only one- to two-pounds each. And it was only then that I realized why these chicks had been free to begin with. They were "broilers" because they were roosters, not hens. But they were not real meat birds, bred for that purpose. They were the almost useless males of breeds which were bred for egg-laying.

I spent a total of $67.60 on these free chicks, whose final weight came to about nine pounds. That comes to $7.51 per pound, just a few pennies more than the 98¢ a pound this type of meat would have cost me at the time at the local supermarket. Truffles would have been a better buy.

Sixty Slices of Life... on Wry

Nevertheless they were good, if not filling. They were very lean. For all the money and work involved in raising our chicks to maturity, I expected the difference in taste to be worth it. I'm not sure it was.

But it was definitely more difficult to eat them without thinking about just a few days before, when they excitedly ran up to me as I approached their enclosure, eagerly anticipating the food and water I was bringing their way. This was not a problem I ever encountered with supermarket chickens.

Perhaps I should have arranged to trade my six freshly packaged chickens for someone else's six freshly packaged chickens? Maybe the Chicken Plucker would start a Chicken Exchange?

Well, I've purchased 12 more chicks—real Cornish Cross meat birds this time. They grow so fast, the Chicken Plucker tells me, that, if they are not processed within 10 weeks, their legs will break from their own weight. They're supposed to taste better, too. I'll know soon enough.

Vegetarian friends say I'm a hypocrite because I don't kill the meat I eat. True, if I had to slaughter my own chickens, I'd probably join their ranks. But I don't think that makes me a hypocrite. I'm just—there's no other word for it—chicken!

• • • •

After reading this true account, my vegetarian daughter accused me of not only exploiting chickens, killing them and eating their meat, but then selling their life story! I plead guilty on all counts!

50
The Hen Who Loved Haydn

Once upon a time, many years ago, when I was a little boy growing up in the highly populated suburbs of New York City, I had a passion for eggs. I loved them soft-boiled, hard-boiled, medium-boiled, poached, sunny-side up, and once-over-lightly. I still do.

In those days, before the word cholesterol had entered the national vocabulary, I could eat all the eggs I wanted, because they were widely believed to be good for you. I had two for breakfast several times a week, and when my kosher grandmother wasn't visiting, they were always accompanied by bacon.

When I was nine years old, I went with my parents during the summer to Connecticut and Massachusetts, where we visited one relative after another, including an aunt and uncle who lived in the country. These relatives had hens, and, one morning, I was treated to the first really fresh, just-out-of-the-chicken eggs I had ever eaten. It was a taste I would never forget.

Almost a half-century later, when my wife and I moved to southern Oregon on 12 acres in the country, I looked forward to having chickens, and, once again—for the first time in all these years—eating fresh, unrefrigerated, direct-from-the-hen eggs.

But, by this time, I had been found to have high cholesterol and was reduced to one egg a week. There was

Sixty Slices of Life... on Wry

certainly no need for me and my wife to have more than one hen.

One day it came to pass that the sudsy water from our washing machine backed up into our basement and we had to call Bill at Speedy Rooter to clear our line. What, you may wonder, does this have to do with chickens and eggs? Well, everything, actually.

You see it turns out that while shooting the breeze with Bill as he snaked the sewer line, I learned that he had some chickens he was about to butcher for meat, including some hens. He promised to save one for me.

Several weeks went by and no hen showed up, when the sewer line backed up again. Once more Bill came to the rescue, only this time he couldn't get his snake to clear the line. It was apparently broken.

Although Bill couldn't fix the problem, and it still cost me $39.50, he at least remembered to bring the hen, which he gave me as a gift. Bill suggested keeping it in the garage with a heat lamp over her head during the winter. Out in the cold, he said, she would stop laying eggs. Bill said this beautiful black hen would give us an egg a day for the next year.

So I went out searching for a cage designed to accommodate a single, solitary hen. When, after extensive research locally and via long-distance telephone, I found out that no such product exists, I purchased a build-it-yourself rabbit cage and adapted it for my new hen. I added a hanging water dish designed for parrots, lined the rabbit feeder with plastic so the finer chicken feed wouldn't fall through the cracks, and designed and built from scratch out of wood a nest in the shape of a bed, complete with headboard.

I placed the new cage on the workbench in the garage, just in front of a built-in stereo speaker, which I turned

Sixty Slices of Life... on Wry

off so that the hen wouldn't be disturbed by the national and international news coming though the house system from the tuner in the living room. My wife named the bird "Noirette."

Each day I fed my new hen and gave her fresh water. This wasn't as easy as it sounds, because Noirette had a very natural tendency to peck at whatever was placed inside her cage. Especially if it moved. It was almost impossible not to spill the water when the hand holding the dish kept getting attacked. What's worse, I took this pecking personally at first, and my self-esteem suffered with each attack.

Later I realized that those twice-a-day cage openings, when a human hand went quickly in and out, were the high points of Noirette's day. Any human hand would have been treated equally, I'm sure. Well, at least, I think. In any case I had become, quite literally, a hen-pecked husband, although my wife was not at all to blame. And it would have been nice if this hen could have learned not to bite the hand that fed it.

Despite all this good care and attention, Noirette wouldn't use her new nest and she didn't lay an egg.

The backhoe man, who came to dig up and replace the broken sewer pipe, thought Noirette might be lonely, and I worried that he was right. But the cage was too small for two chickens, never mind human companionship. And, even if I could have fit inside with her, I didn't like where I obviously fit in her pecking order.

Another day passed and then another, and Noirette still didn't lay an egg. Then I got an idea. I turned on the stereo speaker next to Noirette's cage, keeping the volume down, and put on some compact discs. Carefully selecting this music, it struck me how few composers wrote with an aviary audience in mind. I chose gentle classical music

Sixty Slices of Life... on Wry

by Haydn along with a more spirited piece by Respighi ("The Birds") and, of course, the "Chicken Reel" by Leroy Anderson. I thought the music might serve to keep Noirette company, as it did me during the long, winter days alone at home writing at my computer while my wife was out doing something useful for a living.

The very next morning, Noirette hopped up on her nest, shuffled about restlessly for ten or fifteen minutes, stretched her head up to the top of the cage, made a few soft, strange, high-pitched sounds, and dropped a fresh, warm egg right into the waiting pine-shavings mattress.

I discovered the egg shortly afterwards and, as excited as a nine-year-old, ran into the kitchen where my wife and I had just finished breakfast.

"Let's boil some water!" I shouted, holding the round object high in the air, as proud as if I had laid it myself.

We shared that first egg together, and Noirette dropped another beautiful, big brown egg every morning after that.

Not only that, she was also exposed to Mozart, Beethoven, Tchaikovsky and Mahler! She listened to National Public Radio's *All Things Considered* every afternoon at 5, and the eggs keep coming—despite wars, assassinations and federal deficits. Even Newt Gingrich's budget cuts didn't bother her, independent entrepreneur that she was.

Noirette worked hard for her food, water, shelter and piped-in classical music. It never ceased to amaze me that she could produce such a large, new egg every day. And she did this naturally and organically, without at all harming her environment. She was by far the most useful and productive pet I had ever had.

I wish she could have lived—and laid—happily ever after!

51
Potbellied Pigs ... and Husbands

I was looking though the classified advertisements one day trying to find some inexpensive, used metal file cabinets for my office. I didn't find any, but I did notice an ad for potbellied pigs.

I called the lady who was selling them (only $25 each), reserved two, and told her I would come to pick them up when my wife returned with the car. I had in mind that Laurel and Hardy—as I chose to call them, sight unseen—could join Noirette la Poule and Benjamin Bunny in the Frederic M. Flaxman Memorial Chicken Coop, which I had had professionally built by this time. (I figured that if I didn't name a building after myself, who would?)

But when Annick returned with the car and I told her what I was about to do, she had a fit! She said I didn't know anything about potbellied pigs and that I was like a child, acting on impulse!

Imagine that! Acting on impulse! Who? Me?

The only reason we had chickens then is because I acted rapidly and decisively when I saw that FREE CHICKS sign in front of Morton Feeds & Grains—without having had the opportunity, in that case, to consult with Annick first. Now no one appreciates Noirette's fresh eggs more than my wonderful wife!

You don't see potbellied pigs for sale for $25 each every day! And the lady had sold all but two—both males—

Sixty Slices of Life... on Wry

by the time I called.

I had to act fast. This was an emergency. Annick had to be convinced right away. There wasn't time to go to the library. So I got on the Internet, picked a search engine, typed in "potbellied pigs," and was amazed at how much information came my way on the subject in a matter of seconds.

Particularly useful were the Potbellied Pig Directory and the Official Bacon Links, Life & PBP FAQ. But there was a home page for Miss Piggy, Pig Resources, Piggy Pictures (including one of Hamlet), Critter's Choice Pig Links, a Bacon & Eggs Home Page, one for the National Committee on Potbellied Pigs, and another for the North American Potbellied Pig Association! (One has yet to be created for the North American Potbellied Husbands Association, for which I would certainly qualify as president and chairman of the board. Their motto could be: "Potbellied husbands make great pets.")

I learned that miniature potbellied pigs originated in the jungles of China and Vietnam and were introduced to the U.S. as pets around 1985. "Since that time," the PBP FAQ continues, "the Miniature Potbellied Pig has achieved an ever-growing popularity among pet owners through its general cleanliness, intelligence, and unique appearance."

However, the potbellied pig's "unique appearance" was described elsewhere on the Internet as "the ugliest dog ever seen." That same, apparently honest document goes on to say that "pigs aren't soft or cuddly to touch either, they have spiky hair covering their body, and they have little hooves to walk on, not soft pads like dogs and cats."

The males also grow tusks which need to be snipped off "to avoid the possibility of injury." The piglets needle

Sixty Slices of Life... on Wry

teeth should be trimmed "to prevent injury to the sow or litter mates." And their canine teeth should be removed around four months "to avoid punctures." I also learned that "adult male pigs with all their hormones can be more aggressive and will develop a foul smell."

Somehow, none of this information helped convince Annick that I should go to pick up the two PBPs. She liked the idea even less when she learned that these creatures can live as long as 20 years.

This was followed by a discussion of our finances and where the purchase of these pigs, the vet bills, the food and their housing accommodations fit in our list of priorities.

So I called the lady back, and was never in my life so happy to speak to an answering machine.

Next I sent e-mail messages to some of my friends about the potbellied pigs I didn't buy. This is the kind of earth-shattering, timely, important subject to which e-mail's rapid speed is ideally suited. Peter Bradley, a long-time friend who has lived for many years in the mountains of southern California, e-mailed right back:

"Annick is absolutely right. Congratulations for not getting the pigs. You would have been sorry—even terribly sorry. We recently gave ours away, having bought Beldar at age two months almost three years ago. We delighted in having him—for a while, anyway. But the novelty wore off, especially after he grew his tusks (which we didn't file down) and began to establish his territory.

"We had installed a pigloo for his house, a structure twice his size and which he'd mount occasionally, thinking, I'm sure, it was his wife. Despite being a country boy of sorts, I had never seen a pig's penis. And Beldar flashed his often: a corkscrew!

"When the rains came, he was in pig heaven. When

Sixty Slices of Life... on Wry

he'd dig himself under the fence and escape into the fields or travel as much as a mile to neighbors' yards, he was in ecstasy. And when we gave him away, after a few hundred dollars in feed, he was happily, to me, gone.

"I've been there, Fred. I've done that. You don't need to."

So I called a teenage girl who raised and sold rabbits, and placed an order for a young female to keep Benjamin Bunny company. She cost only $5, and Annick, feeling somewhat guilty about denying my desire to have potbellied pigs, gave her reluctant approval.

52
Mouth-Watering Meatless Meatballs?

I wrote a column for the Ashland, Ore., *Lithiagraph* on why I wasn't a vegetarian, despite all the good arguments for becoming one. Somewhere in there I mentioned that vegetarians seemed to lack a sense of humor.

Shortly afterwards a package arrived in my mailbox from Lumen Foods in Lake Charles, Louisiana. As I was in my late 50s at the time and my short-term memory had been playing tricks on me, I racked my brain to try to remember ordering something from this company—but to no avail.

I was a bit worried about opening a package like this since, by its size and weight, it might have been something a lot less good for my health than food. People who express their views in print have to be particularly careful about opening unordered packages, even though authorities believe they have the Unibomber behind bars. You never know.

So you can imagine my surprise when this turned out to be a most exciting, interesting, and appropriate gift from someone whom I have never met: a package of substitute meats!

Annick and I tried the "jerky" out of the bag first and thought it was quite good. Then we heated it in the microwave for 10 seconds and found it even better.

We next tried the "hamburger" to make a "meat" sauce for spaghetti. This was less successful, as were the

Sixty Slices of Life... on Wry

"hamburgers" Annick tried to make the next day.

We looked forward to experimenting with all the other foods in this CARE package, which couldn't have come at a better time since Annick was trying to give up meat as much as possible, and I was trying to lower my cholesterol.

Then, at about 8:30 p.m. a few evenings later, when Annick was about to start her evening yoga session, I heard a vehicle on our driveway. It was a pick-up truck, the kind frequently used in construction. As we were not expecting any visitors, much less a contractor, and the truck was unfamiliar, I wondered who could have the nerve to come up our long driveway, past our clear NO TRESPASSING, PRIVATE PROPERTY and NO SOLICITING signs, at this time of day.

I went outside on our front porch to see who it was and, to my surprise—not to say amazement—a clown in full circus regalia emerged from the truck and said to me, with a British accent no less:

"I have come to prove that vegetarians have a sense of humor."

He then produced a package of vegan goodies he insisted was for me, and started lighting batons that he proceeded to juggle.

I ran to get my wife so she could see what was going on, and to get my camera.

My wife asked the man's name. We both thought he replied "I'm Tofu the Clown," and we laughed. Later we learned from his business card that he was Toful the Clown, a.k.a. Tony Henthorn. He explained that Toful was short for Tony the Fool.

When Toful put out the fire at the end of each baton by swallowing it, I told him I thought that was carrying vegetarianism a bit far. We invited him in for a fruit juice

Sixty Slices of Life... on Wry

drink, but now that I think of it, water might have gone better with the meal he had consumed.

Tony was a fascinating character and we enjoyed our conversation for an hour or so. He refused to take a tip I tried to offer him on his way out. He said my vegetarian benefactor had amply covered the cost of his services.

The very next day the UPS man came with a package from Dixie USA, Inc. in Houston, Texas. Another box of vegetarian meat substitutes!

I was beginning to have a problem writing thank-you notes as fast as the vegetarian gifts were coming in. If this kept up, I warned my benefactor, I'd never be able to write an article in favor of vegetarianism—for fear of being accused of accepting bribes in return for favorable, perhaps even flavorable, publicity!

But I have to admit that I know at least one vegetarian with an excellent sense of humor as well as a generous heart and, evidently, missionary zeal!

Yet he didn't convert me. But my wife joined his ranks for a while and I served as a guinea pig almost every day as she tried out the food he sent—on the two of us. I wrote my unsolicited vegetarian friend that I would let him know if I survived these experiments and that he'd hear from the lawyer for my estate if I didn't.

I would love to find vegetarian food which I can enjoy as much as meat, but, so far, except for beefless beef jerky, I find that it ranges from bad to not bad, either bland or too spicy. I haven't come across anything that I would call really good, anything that equals the taste of a good filet mignon, much less surpasses it.

In fact I'm afraid the experiment had the opposite of its intended effect. Shortly after the vegetarian packages were all consumed, I stopped for lunch at the Goodtimes

Sixty Slices of Life… on Wry

Café in Ashland and ate one of their thick, juicy, half-pound hamburgers. I don't think I ever appreciated the taste of real meat so much before.

53
Dealing with Dental Guilt

I've become a dental saint. I brush my teeth after every meal—even lunch—and floss every night before going to bed, no matter how late it is or how tired I feel. I use a pricey electric toothbrush recommended by my dentist. And this is how I've behaved ever since my last trip to his office for teeth cleaning and examination.

For me, going to the dentist is the opposite of seeing a psychiatrist. Psychiatrists help alleviate feelings of guilt; dentists instill them. You can go to your dentist feeling good about yourself, your accomplishments, your life—and return home convinced that you will be severely punished with periodontal disease if you consistently fail to floss.

The picture he paints of your future is so bleak, purgatory looks like paradise by comparison. Bleeding gums, decaying teeth, root canal work, crowns, losing your teeth altogether, and—worst of all—unprecedented dental bills are certain to await those who are too busy to brush or not fastidious enough to floss.

And all this is almost literally drilled into you while you are confined to the dentist's chair and he picks away at your tartar-filled nooks and crevices. He has a captive audience—you—and a half hour or so of your undivided attention while you stare up at the ceiling with nothing better to do than to count the acoustic tiles.

Sixty Slices of Life... on Wry

"Have you been flossing?" my dentist asked on my last visit, as he asks on every visit.

"I refuse to answer on the grounds that my reply might tend to incriminate me," I retorted, hoping that the Fifth Amendment would protect me if all of a sudden the dentist's chair became, as it so often does, electric.

But dentists know when you haven't been flossing. And when you haven't listened to their previous admonitions, they have ways of getting back at you. Dr. Smalowitz, my previous dentist, used to send in his most sadistic dental assistant to scrape at my teeth until my gums bled and I swore on my gold fillings that I would floss each day for the rest of my life. That's why Dr. Smalowitz is my previous dentist.

My current dentist is such a nice guy, I feel even more guilty when I visit him. How could I possibly present this college educated, clean cut, middle class, decent doctor of dentistry with such a dirty, plaque-infested, tartar-ridden mouth? Is he wearing thin rubber gloves because he is worried about getting AIDS, or is he just protecting himself from the filthy mouths of the great unflossed?

I've read that dentists have the highest suicide rate of any profession. I can understand why. Day after day they look into cigarette-stained orifices, fill cavities, inject Novocain, and deal with screaming kids. The kids alone would drive most people mad. Their job is like pulling teeth. In fact, it is pulling teeth.

But then again, dentists charge a lot more than other people whose job it is to clean something. Garbage men, for example, remove considerably more waste twice a week than dental assistants do twice a year. And how much do they make? Or maids? Or waiters?

Still, I wouldn't want to spend eight hours a day

Sixty Slices of Life... on Wry

doing what dentists have to do to make a living, no matter how good a living they make. Maybe they do charge what the traffic will bear. They deserve what they get.

Nevertheless there are a few things dentists could do to make me less likely to postpone my next appointment:

1. Install high definition TV monitors in their ceilings and give me a choice of adult videos to play so that I'd have something more interesting than medical equipment and ceiling tiles to look at when I'm propped back in their chairs.

2. Learn to talk about something more exciting than gum disease.

3. Develop a cholesterol-free, non-fattening, chocolate-flavored mouthwash cleanser I could swish around once or twice a day that would accomplish everything that the most proficient brushing and flossing does now, only do it better.

54
Sharing the Fruit of Our Labor

When my wife and I moved to Palm Beach County, we purchased an 18-year-old house on 1.2 acres. We were more attracted to the park-like landscape than we were to the house itself. We especially liked the large citrus grove. There were orange, grapefruit, tangerine, lemon, and lime trees—19 in all—producing far more than enough fruit for the two of us. It may not have been exactly our dream house, but it was our Garden of Eden.

We expected to share our bounty with friends and relatives, but were realistic enough to foresee a certain percentage going to the local wildlife that lived in the three acres of woods immediately behind the house.

We moved into our new home in November, just as the first tangerines of the season were coming "on line." By the time the first oranges started ripening, Annick began each day by picking up the discarded peels of about twenty of them right under and around the tree that was ready for harvesting. Although we were willing to share our produce with the raccoons, their idea of a fair split was 90% for them, 10% for us.

These masked bandits were taking off with so much of our fruit, we started to worry that we were going to lose almost our whole crop to them. They were getting more and more brazen about it, too. A couple of months passed before we ever saw one during the day. But the riper and

Sixty Slices of Life… on Wry

sweeter the fruit we had on our trees, the more raccoons we saw during the day and evening. After another month went by, they seemed to have three shifts alternating around the clock.

I encountered raccoons in the citrus trees more and more often when I went outside to harvest some fruit. They got down very quickly when I approached, making a mad dash for the woods, never stopping to look back. Except for one. At least I think he was the same one. He was bigger than the rest and more sure of himself. He would trot exactly half way from the citrus grove to the woods, stop, turn around and look at me as if to say, "You're never going to get me!" after which he would complete his return to the complete safety of the dense, jungle-like little Florida forest.

"There must be a huge population of raccoons in the woods," I said to my spouse. "After all, our predecessors helped create an ideal environment for them: housing and water in the woods [where there is a pond] and all the food they could imagine, served to them every evening promptly at six. For desert there was a selection of delicious, tree-ripened fruit to munch on to their hearts' content at a convenient, outdoor restaurant, open 24 hours a day."

With our bountiful harvest disappearing faster than we could squeeze fresh orange juice, we decided something must be done—quickly. But what? I called Palm Beach County Animal Control to find out.

"Press 1 for cats, 2 for dogs," the answering machine replied, continuing with a menu of options which included neither raccoons nor live humans I could ask about raccoons. Eventually I reached a live operator.

"We don't handle raccoons," she told me. "You'll have to call a wild animal trapper. They're in the phone book."

Sixty Slices of Life... on Wry

"But what do they do with the raccoons they catch?" I asked.

"They euthanize them," she replied, as though that meant putting them to bed for a good night's sleep rather than killing them.

"What if I trap them myself?"

"Then you can bring them here and we'll euthanize them for $20 each."

Raccoons, in case you don't know, are about the size of huge cats. They are greyish brown and white with black stripes on their tails and they look as though they are wearing a black mask over their eyes. They are as cute as can be, which is their best defence against softies like me. If there were rats this size on my property, I'm sure I would not have hesitated to call in the exterminator and had them euthanized—or even murdered—as quickly as possible. Rats, after all, can bite. They can carry rabies. They're dangerous.

Well, so are raccoons. But they're so adorable! Besides, at $20 a shot, it could be pretty expensive to take care of our problem. And that's the cheap way, without calling in a pro.

I thanked the one human being I could reach at Animal Control, and went out and purchased a live trap.

For the next month I operated a private limousine service for raccoons, transporting them one at a time to a Florida Department of Conservation nature reserve exactly 4.2 miles from our garage door. There was a creature in the trap/cage every morning, and sometimes a second one in the evening. We kept count and I turned the whole experience into a math lesson for our nine-year-old granddaughter.

"I purchased the raccoon trap for $32," I told her. "If

Sixty Slices of Life... on Wry

I caught just one raccoon with this trap, how much would that raccoon have cost me, not counting the price of the peanut butter I used as bait or the gasoline it took to transport him to the nature reserve?"

"Thirty-two dollars," she replied.

"Good. Now let's say I caught two raccoons in that $32 trap. How much would it have cost to capture each raccoon?"

This was the first division problem she had ever encountered, I think, and she had no idea what the answer was. So I taught her, and every day we had a new lesson in division and amortization as the cost per raccoon kept coming down and down.

That month we captured 22 raccoons, two possums and one small red fox at a cost of only $1.28 per creature, not including the funds expended for five jars of peanut butter, 12 apples, and 14 pieces of Annick's leftover sushi.

I learned that raccoons are like French people: They'll eat anything. Although, unlike most French people, they'll even devour the cardboard or plastic container you use to feed them. However, they are very clever critters. Sushi didn't work, not because they didn't like it, but because they could manage to get it *out* of the trap without going *in* the trap. Cardboard *à la mode* with peanut butter on top turned out to be the most effective bait.

I stopped trapping after a month for two reasons: (1) We were totally out of fruit; (2) I found out that I was a criminal.

I was never sure I was operating totally within the law because there was a *No Trespassing* sign at the entrance to the nature preserve and I went a dozen or so feet beyond that sign to deposit my passengers. Although I did this most often late at night under the cover of darkness, I did wonder

Sixty Slices of Life... on Wry

what my defense would be if and when I were caught.

One day it occurred to me that every previous *No Trespassing* sign I could remember seeing also contained the words "Private Property." This one said: "Park Boundary, NO TRESPASSING, Florida Dept. of Natural Resources."

This was not private property. It was public property, owned by the residents of the state of Florida. I was one of the owners. Therefore I was not trespassing as it is not possible to be a trespasser on one's own property! Besides, it was a park devoted to natural resources, and resources don't come more natural than raccoons.

I almost got to test out this legal theory late one evening just as I was putting my empty trap/cage back in my station wagon after having taxied Raccoon No. 14 to the nature reserve. A police car came up from behind and a bright spotlight swerved from the roof of the car and aimed directly at me, making me feel instantly like a criminal caught in the act.

"What are you trapping?" the police officer asked?

"I'm not trapping anything," I replied truthfully. "I'm just returning to nature a creature that belongs in nature."

"O.K.," the officer replied, without asking what kind of creature I had put back in nature or how many of them I had put back before. "Have a good evening," he said and he drove on.

I should have been arrested, it turns out, but not for trespassing. Unbeknownst to me, I had violated a state law against transporting wildlife. Although the law was put on the books to prevent the commercial exploitation and sale of wildlife and wasn't intended to prevent homeowners from removing raccoons from their own property, it was poorly written and provided for no exemption for homeowners.

As there is no law against trapping raccoons on your

Sixty Slices of Life... on Wry

own property, but there is a law against moving them, the Palm Beach County homeowner's options for solving this animal pest problem is rather limited. You can trap them and euthanize them on the spot or you can trap them and kill them on the spot. Anyway you put it, in Palm Beach County, the only good raccoon is a dead raccoon.

The following August the fruit, once again, was growing on our citrus trees. I was hoping that we'd have plenty to share with our friends and relatives the following winter as there should have been 22 fewer raccoons and their offspring living in the vicinity. I hadn't seen a raccoon in my yard all summer. Then one day, looking out from our patio towards the woods in back, I saw an extra-large size coon trotting from the citrus grove to the little forest.

He stopped about half way, turned around and looked towards me with what I could swear was a sneering expression on his masked face. Then he continued his journey into the woods.

I knew he'd be back, and that he'd bring his family, friends, and relatives when he returned.

Sixty Slices of Life... on Wry

55
Speeding to Success

I'm an optimist by nature. So, looking back on my first year in Florida, I would conclude that I made a living as a freelance writer and earned enough money to pay the bills. Just barely. Pessimists might say that I was unemployed—without even the benefits of unemployment insurance. And it is true that I was trying to find a full-time job from the moment I arrived, without success.

Without success, that is, until, on May 26, 1999, I received a ticket for speeding. This citation led to the very job I wanted most at the time: working, once again, for a public broadcasting organization.

Before I even moved to Palm Beach County I sent a letter to the CEO of WXEL-TV-FM, the local public broadcasting outlets, inquiring about a job. When I arrived, the top two executives of the nonprofit outfit spent an hour with me, but there were no openings suitable for someone with my background and experience. Six months later, when I inquired again, the situation hadn't changed.

Then, on May 26, I was returning to my house from the town just west of us on a part of a road I had never been on before. It was a straight, two-lane country road with no development on either side, no ingresses or egresses and no cross streets. There wasn't even livestock on the sides. It was the kind of thoroughfare where the speed limit everywhere else in the U.S., and even everywhere else in Florida, is 55 miles per hour. But the speed limit here was only 40, and there was one sign, which I failed to notice, indicating as much.

However, as the road went further east, cross streets began to appear, as well as housing developments and even an elementary school. The road became four lanes divided, then six. And, strangely enough, the more people, the more houses, the more pets and the more children in the area, the faster the speed limit became. From 40 it went to 45 and then, as it got close to my home where I was familiar with the road, the speed limit was set at 55.

Officer Camargo was seated in his patrol car with his radar going at the point where the speed limit went from 40 to 45. I'm sure this wasn't the first time that he parked there, nor would it be the last. He handed me a ticket for going 60 m.p.h. in a 40 m.p.h. zone. Much to my surprise, the fine would be $160. That's a lot of money for a struggling freelance writer or for someone who's unemployed, looking for a job. I decided to fight it.

The system encourages you to plead guilty and send in your check by mail. If you take your case to court and are found guilty, you are warned, you may have to pay an even larger fine, plus court costs. But, as I thought this speed trap was unfair and unjust, and I could go to court without losing a day's pay (one of the many advantages of being either a freelance writer or unemployed), I decided I would take that chance. Besides, I remembered that if Officer Camargo didn't show up in traffic court for any reason on the day of my hearing, I would automatically win my case and have nothing at all to pay. And I also remembered that the last ticket I had received for speeding, some 16 years earlier in Chicago, was thrown out for everyone who bothered to show up at the courthouse that morning. So I had hope.

My day in court came on August 11. I was well pre-

Sixty Slices of Life... on Wry

pared. I had gone over the road, carefully noting conditions and speed limits. I had my testimony written out in advance. (That is something else you can do if you have the skills of a freelance writer and the time availability of the unemployed.)

"Your honor," I began, "I pleaded not guilty to the traffic offense I have been charged with because I know that this is a court of justice and I wanted to bring to your attention what I think is an unjust situation that affects many other people besides me." I went on to describe the situation in detail and hoped that the lady magistrate would hear me out to my conclusion.

"The point I am trying to make is not that I wasn't exceeding the posted speed limit," I confessed, "but rather that the speed limits themselves are unjust and illogical and are perhaps the very opposite of what they should be. The more inhabited the area, the more ingresses and egresses, the more developed the area is, the more children may be present... the faster cars are permitted to go. Does that make sense?"

Well it wasn't in the magistrate's power to order Palm Beach County to change the speed limit. She said that she didn't make the law, but that she was sworn to uphold it and that she had no choice but to find me guilty.

I braced myself for the worst, starting to worry that she would actually raise the fine in retaliation for my wasting the court's time on so frivolous a case. Annick, who was sitting in the audience, heard snickering behind her.

But the magistrate checked the computer for prior violations and didn't find any, so she charged me $10 for court costs and gave me the choice of paying the $160 fine or doing 16 hours of community service. Being a freelance writer or unemployed, depending on how you look at it,

Sixty Slices of Life... on Wry

the 16 hours were no problem and the $160 were, so I went to the next room to look through a large notebook of community service opportunities.

Did I want to do yard work for the Catholic church? Well, no, not exactly. This was August in south Florida and I had enough lawn mowing and cleanup to do in my own yard. Besides I'm not Catholic and I don't like to sweat.

Did I want to paint the Institute for Young Drug Offenders or clean the bathrooms at the Home for Unwed Mothers? Not particularly. Weren't there any less strenuous, indoor, office-work type assignments I could do?

Then I got an idea. I looked up the local public broadcasting outfit to see if they were listed, and sure enough they were! And it turned out WXEL-TV was right in the middle of one of their on-air membership drives and in need of volunteers to answer the phones and take pledges. They even fed the volunteers! This was the ideal way for me to put in my 16 hours—especially the eating. I do that anyway, all day long. What do you think freelance writers and the unemployed do with their not-so-spare time?

As luck would have it the CEO of WXEL-TV was there the very first night I came in. And so was the Director of Development. Between the on-air fund-raising sessions, the Director of Development talked to the CEO and then came over and asked me to meet with her the next day to discuss the possibility of my working for the station. When I passed the CEO on the way out of the studio, I said to him that I really hadn't come to the station looking for a job this time. He said he knew that, but that since our last contact, someone had resigned, opening up a spot which might make a good match for my abilities.

And that's how, thanks to Officer Camargo and a sympathetic magistrate, I became Vice President for Development of WXEL.

Sixty Slices of Life… on Wry

56
Dressing Appropriately

In 2005 WXEL was owned by Barry University. For several months the University had been mulling over proposals it solicited to transfer the public radio and television stations where I worked to some other institution.

On Thursday, March 31, at about 3:30 P.M., Jerry Carr, the station's president and CEO, announced that there would be an all-staff meeting at 11:00 A.M. the next day, after which he promptly left the building.

I assumed that Barry University had finally made its decision on which nonprofit would be the next owner of WXEL, and that this would be announced to the staff then. Others made the same assumption and quickly looked into Jerry's office to see if he had cleaned it out before he left.

Fridays were dress-down days at WXEL, meaning that you could dress very informally and comfortably. Jerry usually wore a T-shirt over his hefty frame, setting the standard for that day of the week.

On April 1, I dressed as usual for a Friday meeting, with a nice sport shirt and comfortable khakis. Not long after I arrived at the station, where I was serving as vice-president for development, Jerry called me into his office for a meeting with the president of Barry and a few others, all of whom, including Jerry, were dressed in ties and jackets or the female equivalent.

Sister Linda Bevelaqua, Barry's president, then ex-

Sixty Slices of Life... on Wry

plained Barry's decision to us, which, as it turned out, she had done to Jerry by phone the day before.

Sensing that she might have trouble convincing me that their decision was the right one, she looked at me straight in the eyes as she spoke. I hoped that she was concentrating so intently on what she was saying that she didn't notice my tie-less attire.

The sale was going to be to WNET/13, New York City's public television station.

We then proceeded to move to WXEL's board room, where we were joined by the president, vice president, and financial officer of WNET. Also in the room were members of WXEL's board of trustees. There again, everyone was dressed to the hilt.

No one said anything about the way I was dressed, of course, but I felt very embarrassed. It made me think of a nightmare I had many years earlier in which I found myself in the middle of a well-dressed crowd someplace wearing nothing but my birthday suit.

Sister Linda explained Barry's decision once again. Then Bill Baker, WNET's president at the time, elaborated on why he thought this would be such a good idea for both WNET and WXEL. A few WXEL board members asked questions. Jerry Carr said how pleased he was with Barry's decision. WXEL's vice president for finances, ever the diplomat, agreed with Jerry, and it was my turn to say a few words.

I also expressed support for the deal, but added that I had one very serious concern.

Jerry and Sister Linda looked very worried about what I might say next. Would I say something that would muck up the deal? Would I bring up a point that no one

Sixty Slices of Life... on Wry

had considered and which would make the sale impossible to consummate?

"Bill Baker said that things would stay the same at WXEL, or get better," I said with all the force I could muster so that everyone in the room could hear me. "We have been assured that no staff changes were anticipated, since the staff has been doing such a good job. We would be joining forces with the nation's preeminent public television station, with an organization whose mission parallels our own and is devoted to public broadcasting.

"But," I added, then paused to build the tension in the room. "I'm concerned about continuing WXEL's traditions under the new ownership. For example, Friday is dress-down day at WXEL and, looking around the room, I see that I am the only person here who is appropriately dressed for the occasion."

Everyone burst out laughing and breathed a collective sigh of relief. The tension in the room disappeared, and I felt a little less embarrassed about how I was dressed.

The following Monday Jerry told me how happy he was that I had worn casual clothes to those meetings. "Sister Linda made me promise on Thursday when she phoned not to tell a soul, not even my vice-presidents. The way you dressed proved without a doubt that I had kept my word."

(Lacking the approval of the Federal Communications Commission, the sale of WXEL to WNET fell through more than two years later. It was said that the FCC wanted to preserve local ownership of public broadcasting stations. I think it was because they wanted to preserve dress-down Fridays.)

••••

Sixty Slices of Life... on Wry

The following Monday, as luck would have it, I had jury duty. In Palm Beach County potential jurors need to call before reporting to the courthouse. An answering device gives them recorded instructions. These include dressing "in business attire." I took that to mean ties and jackets for men.

There were a couple of hundred people in the auditorium set aside for prospective jurors. About half of them were women. There were some young, very attractive women who were wearing very low cut tops with very short skirts. I could only speculate on what business they might have been in.

But there wasn't another man in that large, crowded room—not one single man aside from me—who was wearing a tie or jacket.

For the second time in less than a week I was the only person in the room who was appropriately dressed. This time it didn't matter at all. I sat there and read the entire day without ever being called to sit on a jury, thankful that I was not held in contempt of court for my non-conforming dress.

Sixty Slices of Life... on Wry

57
Selecting the Worst President in History

I have a confession to make. I am personally responsible for George W. Bush becoming president of the United States of America. I'm not joking, and I am truly sorry for what I did, but I'll try to explain to you exactly how it happened.

Think back to the year 2000 when George W. Bush was the Republican candidate and Albert Gore was the Democratic choice. There was also a Green Party nominee for president. His name was Ralph Nader. And this was the year of the infamous "butterfly ballot" in Palm Beach County, Florida, as well as the "hanging chad."

My wife and I lived in Palm Beach County at the time, and we voted on the butterfly ballot, she in one booth, I in the next. We emerged at the same time and said to each other that that ballot was very confusing because the names on the left page didn't line up properly with the punch holes on the right.

"Old folks are really going to have problems in the voting booth," I said to my wife, "even if their eyesight isn't failing."

"Yes, really," she replied. "Even I found that confusing and I'm not that old yet."

She voted for Al Gore. I voted for ...

Well Ralph Nader was one of my heroes. His views on just about everything corresponded to my own. And he was as honest a person as I could imagine with a personal

Sixty Slices of Life… on Wry

history of courageous reform. He was just the kind of individual I've always felt we needed as president of the U.S. Yet I knew he didn't have a chance of winning, and I also liked Al Gore.

My wife had read Al Gore's book on the environment and was very impressed with him.

"How could you waste your vote for Nader," she asked, "when you know he's not going to win?"

I replied that I had been waiting all my life to vote for someone like him, and that I wanted to vote my conscience since the election was not going to be decided by one vote in Palm Beach County, Florida.

Unfortunately some 540 people thought exactly the way I did and, as it turned out, the election was decided by my vote—and theirs—with a little help from the Supreme Court and the butterfly ballot.

••••

My wife tried to console our daughter and me on the outcome of that election.

"How much harm can George W. and the Republicans really do in two years," she asked, "until we vote to elect our representatives again?"

She said that before Bush invaded Iraq.

Two years later she had her tragic answer. Four years later it was even worse, and yet Bush was elected then as well. I learned my lesson and didn't vote for Nader in 2004. But the American people didn't learn theirs.

••••

At one point during Bush's first term I was manager on duty during one of WXEL's countless public TV fund drives. That meant that I had to stay late that night at the TV station in case a high-level decision were required on any subject during the membership drive. Most of the time you just ended up watching what was going on in the studio.

The very first time I had manager duty, an elderly lady volunteer who had been answering a pledge phone, got up during a break and fell off the pledge phone platform, having not noticed the edge. It was my decision to call an ambulance and to send her flowers and a get-well card the next day in hopes that she wouldn't sue the station.

But on this occasion, the evening was proceeding without incident and I was bored, having no decisions to make or anything else to do.

The program taking up the bulk of the night was a pledge special featuring Yanni at the Acropolis in Athens. To get an appropriate group of volunteers to answer the phones, our volunteer coordinator called a Greek Orthodox priest in West Palm Beach and asked him to bring 12 of his parishioners. He did.

And he had nothing to do either.

So I said to myself that the evening would pass a bit more rapidly if I engaged him in conversation.

"Father," I said, even though I knew he wasn't my father and felt uncomfortable addressing him that way, "I have never in my life had the opportunity to talk to a genuine, orthodox Greek Orthodox priest before and there's a question I would like to ask you."

Flaxman, I said to myself, *you're really going to put your foot in your mouth, you know. You shouldn't bring up this subject.* But I went on anyway, because I was curious, and whatever happened would be more interesting than any alternative I could think of.

"What is it?" he asked.

"Well, I'm not a Christian and I don't pretend to know

Sixty Slices of Life... on Wry

anything about Christianity, but didn't Christ teach to love your neighbor? Didn't he even teach to love your enemy? If that's the case," I went on, "how does George W. Bush get away with calling himself a Christian?"

The priest's answer surprised me. "I agree with you," he said, "and I'll tell you the truth. I voted for Bush in 2000 and I would never vote for him again. I chose Bush because one issue was very important to me and I agreed with him on that. But I learned that you shouldn't judge any candidate for president on just one subject, no matter how vital it is to you, because there are many other things that are important to you and the country, too."

"Was that one issue abortion?" I asked.

"Yes, it was," he replied, and our conversation continued for a couple more hours. But I can't remember what we discussed after that.

What I will never forget, however, is that George W. Bush continued to call himself a Christian and he continued to love his neighbors and his enemies in Iraq by killing and maiming them for the remainder of his presidency.

Could I have prevented this by not voting for Ralph Nader in 2000? Would the other 540 people who voted for him in Palm Beach County that year still have voted for him anyway? Maybe so. But I still couldn't help feeling at least partially guilty for George W. Bush's reign of terror.

So I ordered "Impeach Bush & Cheney" bumper stickers and put them on the front and back of both of our cars. That didn't have the desired result, but at least I tried to feel a little bit less guilty.

••••

One of our recent U.S. presidents had a sexual affair that adversely affected his wife, his daughter, his mistress and himself—four people. Another invaded Iraq—a country which was no threat to the U.S.—based on lies, deceits and bad information—which led to the deaths of literally thousands of innocent people and the destruction of a foreign country. This same born-again Christian president loved his enemies so much, he approved torturing them.

The first president was guilty of the lowest of low crimes—lying about sex. The second was guilty of the highest crimes—murdering men, women, children, our Constitution, and our nation's reputation throughout the world, not to mention getting our country billions of dollars in debt.

Guess which president was impeached.

58
In Defense of Dishwashing

The only culinary art I've ever mastered is dishwashing. Since retiring from full-time employment in public broadcasting, I've had a lot of time to practice.

Dishwashing may not be as much fun as sex, as much exercise as jogging, or as relaxing as a whirlpool bath, but it does have its advantages:

Like sex, dishwashing is most enjoyable when it's not performed routinely three times a day, and is both dirty and clean, depending on how you look at it.

Like jogging, it keeps you on your feet and facilitates creative daydreaming. But unlike running, you can do it comfortably no matter what the weather is like outside. And there is much less chance of keeling over with a heart attack. In fact, dishwashing never killed anyone, even though most people avoid it like the plague.

Like whirlpool baths, dishwashing permits you to play with hot water and soapy suds. And there is no law against doing it in the nude, although I'll admit it's not common practice, and I wouldn't tell my neighbors, if I were you.

Dishwashing helps instill the democratic values of our society. It promotes the equality of men and women. And it is particularly effective at taking high-ranking, overly-paid, over-bearing, over-confident corporate executives and reducing them to humble household hired hands

Sixty Slices of Life… on Wry

and bumbling, glass-breaking blockheads.

Dishwashing—like reading, writing, speaking, and composing great music—separates human beings from the lower forms of life. There is some question as to whether certain animals speak, but none has ever been found who washes dishes.

For those who spend their days doing mental work in offices, dishwashing supplies a righteous, routine, thoughtless activity that gives the brain a badly-needed after-dinner rest. It's Western Civilization's equivalent of contemplating your navel or repeating your mantra.

Even after all these years of women in the work force, most wives who bring home the bacon still cook it. Dishwashing is easier than cooking, and yet many wives, like mine, who do all the meal preparation will accept after-dinner clean-up by their husbands as "doing their share" of the household chores.

Dishwashing would probably be even easier if it weren't for dishwashing machines. These force you to rinse the dishes thoroughly before you put them in, so what sticks to the plates won't get permanently baked in by the intense heat of the dry cycle. They don't seem to work for pots and pans, which are the only cooking utensils which are tough to clean anyway. You also have to eliminate anything made with wood which can crack, thin plastics which might melt, narrow pieces which can fall through the basket and jam the motor, things that are too big to fit, and cups that hold water in their concave bottoms when they are turned upside down. That excludes virtually everything. And then you have to spend too much time trying to figure out how to pack what's left into one load, so as not to waste soap, water, and electricity.

With as many pluses as dishwashing has, I wonder

Sixty Slices of Life... on Wry

why it usually receives such a bad press, or no press at all. Well, I've been wondering long enough. I'd better finish this and go wash the dishes.

59
Exorcising the Evil Cholesterol Spirits

Once upon a time doctors used blood-letting to get rid of evil spirits. Their patients had great faith in them, even though the price of treatment was often a bit excessive. They paid with their lives.

Well, as the French say, the more things change, the more they're the same. I go every six months to a general practitioner in Weaverville, N.C., not a witch doctor in the African bush. But there isn't much difference. What he does is to send me down the hall where the nurses do very much what a sorcerer would have done. Only the words they use are different. They stick a needle in my vein and blood oozes into a vial. It looks like old-fashioned blood-letting to me.

Instead of showing the red liquid to trolls or elves, they send it to an exotic laboratory where—for an exorbitant amount of money—they perform some mysterious rites on it and determine that my body is inhabited by many evil spirits. Too many. A few years ago they found 299 of them, to be exact.

Of course my doctor doesn't call these "evil spirits," because that wouldn't sound very modern or justify the use of high-tech, expensive equipment. Instead, he speaks of "cholesterol."

Like spirits, cholesterol comes in two types: angelic and evil. The bad cholesterol must be reduced, the doctor

Sixty Slices of Life... on Wry

says, or I could be struck down at any moment by a heart attack or stroke. A witch doctor would have said that the evil spirits inhabiting my body must be exorcised or I would fall victim to a curse.

So, having at least as much faith in modern medicine as so-called primitive people have in magicians, I agreed to undergo the rights of exorcism. I stopped eating foods that a special clan of contemporary conjurers, called nutritionists, have determined are inhabited by too many of these demons. I sacrificed eating pigs, cows, and chicken eggs, though an occasional low-cholesterol frog or lizard was OK. I made a daily ritual of eating herbs and fibers, especially a magical essence called oat bran. And I swallowed a little tablet each evening that sent angels or anti-devils or something into my blood to fight and destroy the evil cholesterol wherever it was. I was grateful they did this quietly, so I could sleep.

I became a true believer, there's no doubt. I accepted on complete and utter faith my doctor's word that cholesterol exists, even though I have never seen, heard, or smelt one. Chances are he's never encountered one either.

I believed unquestioningly the laboratory report that I had too many of these little devils in my blood. I had complete faith in the M.D. when he told me that I had a high risk of dying at any moment if I didn't drastically change my lifestyle and eating habits, even though I had never felt better in my life. And I believed with almost religious fervor in the little pill I had to take each day even though it could have been a placebo, for all the apparent effects it had on my body. At more than one dollar each, I *had* to believe that these pills were doing some good.

Every six months I go back to my modern medicine man and have my blood (and money) drawn again.

Sixty Slices of Life... on Wry

Each time he sends the red liquid out to the little elves in Purgatory or Lavatory or wherever they are, and lists of incomprehensible numbers come back a couple of days later which only a witch can decipher.

The last time I went to the doctor he told me that some of the evil spirits had left my body, but I still had many more than was good for my health. If I refrained from ingesting all the things I love most and kept swallowing that pricey pill every night for the rest of my life, I might keep the demons and heart attacks at bay. But, if I really wanted to get my bad cholesterol down to what he considered to be a safe level, I'd have to double the dose of the mega buck little pill ... and, I guess, give up eating altogether.

I continue to make my culinary and financial sacrifices to the Great Devil Cholesterol, and hope that I may be miraculously delivered from his vengeance.

In the meantime, I can't help but think that witch doctors were not so off-the-wall, after all.

60
A Shocking Discovery

When I was a student in Paris many years ago, I often took the Paris Metro, the city's comprehensive subway system. When I was lucky enough to get a seat in a crowded train, I would always offer it gallantly to an old lady or man who looked as if he was not long for this earth and would have trouble standing when the wheels began to roll and the car began to shake.

Fast forward to a more recent trip from North Carolina to Paris. I was in the subway in the French capital once again and all the seats were taken. By chance I was standing right next to an attractive young woman with a low-cut dress seated on a bench. I was almost thrown in her lap when the train took off.

I kept looking at her because she was young, well endowed, sexy, and I didn't have that much choice, considering the crowded circumstances.

When she looked up at me and began to talk to me in her cool, sweet French voice, I felt I was a student once again. And it was spring. And it was Paris. But it was so noisy in the car that I had to bend close to her face and other features to hear what she was saying.

"Sir, would you like a seat?"

My heart sank. I realized all of a sudden that I had completed the cycle of Parisian life, from seat offerer to seat offeree.

Sixty Slices of Life... on Wry

"No thanks," I replied, suffering more from wounded ego than from sore feet.

As if that weren't bad enough, the next day the same situation repeated itself, only this time with a young male student. It was no accident. One eight-hour flight from the U.S. to France had turned me into an old man who looked as if he was not long for this earth and would have trouble standing when the wheels began to roll and the car began to shake.

French friends and relatives were delighted to hear afterwards that there were still polite young people and good manners in France. Well, that may be, but I would never have been insulted like that in the New York subway!

www.ingramcontent.com/pod-product-compliance
Lightning Source LLC
Chambersburg PA
CBHW071309110426
42743CB00042B/1232